Essex County Council

D0177325

Mindfulness titles available from Sheldon Press:

Alcohol Recovery
Catherine G. Lucas

Anxiety and Depression
Dr Cheryl Rezek

Compassion
Caroline Latham

Keeping a Journal
Philip Cowell

Pain Management
Dr Cheryl Rezek

Quit Smoking
Dr Cheryl Rezek

Stress
Philip Cowell and Lorraine Millard

A full list of titles is available from Sheldon Press, 36 Causton Street, London SW1P 4ST and on our website at www.sheldonpress.co.uk

The Mindful Way

Alcohol Recovery

CATHERINE G. LUCAS

First published in Great Britain in 2017

Sheldon Press
36 Causton Street
London SW1P 4ST
www.sheldonpress.co.uk

British Library Cataloguing-in-Publication Data
A catalogue record for this book is available from the British Library

ISBN 978-1-84709-429-2
eBook ISBN 978-1-84709-430-8

Typeset by Fakenham Prepress Solutions, Fakenham, Norfolk NR21 8NN
First printed in Great Britain by Ashford Colour Press
Subsequently digitally reprinted in Great Britain

eBook by Fakenham Prepress Solutions, Fakenham, Norfolk NR21 8NN

Produced on paper from sustainable forests

For Amanda
and all those committed to
healing the wounds of alcoholism.

Also for J. M. and R. S.

Contents

Acknowledgements viii
Note to the reader x
Introduction xi

Part 1: How does mindfulness help?
1 Craving or longing? 3
2 From self-harm to self-care 12
3 Staying on track 27

Part 2: The mindfulness practices
Introduction to the practices 41

4 A first taste of mindfulness 45
5 The classics 55
6 Specific recovery practices 65
7 Everyday mindfulness 74
8 Mindful movement 83

Useful addresses and resources 91
References and further reading 93

Acknowledgements

There is so much to be grateful for in writing a book: the opportunity to help you, the reader; the opportunity to share the wonders of mindfulness; and, of course, the opportunity simply to do what I love – to write. My thanks to the whole Sheldon Press team, especially Fiona Marshall, for this opportunity. Writing about alcohol recovery has been a healing journey for me.

I'm particularly grateful to all those who have contributed. Thank you Ben, Brendan and Richard for undauntedly sharing your stories. They bring the book to life and make the journey of recovery real. I know they will help readers enormously. With courage, you show that recovery is achievable, wounds can be healed.

Thank you also to Dr Paramabandhu Groves, Director of Breathing Space, and Devin Ashwood, of Action on Addiction, for sharing your expertise. Thank you for the incredibly valuable work you do. Of my ever-supportive friends, I'd like to thank Isabel in particular. Many thanks for the generous loan of your home while you were abroad – it makes the perfect writing retreat.

It's wonderful to have my husband-cum-sub-editor by my side when I'm away working on the final stage of a book. Thank you, Swithin, for giving of yourself so freely. The meditative quality of our time away together as we worked on this mindfulness manuscript was precious.

Lastly, I'd like to thank you, the reader. You're the *raison d'être* for these chapters. Without you there would be no book. Certain books have made a huge difference to my life and I hope this one touches yours in the same way.

Note to the reader

No names have been changed or identities hidden, as Ben, Brendan and Richard quite rightly feel that they have nothing to hide and nothing to be ashamed of. Together we can help break down the taboo and stigma around the wounding that leads to alcohol abuse.

Introduction

Mindfulness saved me from alcoholism.

Catherine

My story

I come from a family of alcoholics. A lineage that stretches as far back as a great-grandparent and, for all I know, further still. I've witnessed both the misery of alcoholism and the miracle of recovery.

My father died young, at 49, of throat cancer, relatively common among alcoholics. His short life began in September 1939; he was born just two weeks after the Second World War broke out. His own father died when he was two and he was brought up in the kind of wartime poverty most of us in the West today can only begin to imagine. He won a scholarship to a good school and went on to university. He then worked his way up the career ladder, driven by the kind of ambition poverty fuels. His drinking career and his professional career went hand in hand as he moved up the echelons of the drinks industry, from travelling sales rep for a whisky label to international marketing director of a high street brand of gin. He was a charismatic man but also highly sensitive, and I suspect he struggled in the macho business environment.

While he was the primary addicted person in my life, there were alcoholics on both sides of my family. My mother's brother, my uncle, died of liver disease. Today, I feel so blessed that my generation have found our way to healing, a healing that our parents and grandparents were not fortunate enough to find. I have a huge sense of gratitude for having escaped from the misery of active addiction. I could so easily have followed in my father's footsteps. I look back now at times when I was abusing alcohol and realize what a close escape I had.

As a teenager I would sit in my bedroom listening to Simon and Garfunkel. I would sing along to their song 'I am a rock'. I wanted to be that rock, feeling no pain; I wanted to be the island that never cried. In my late teens and early twenties, as a student, without realizing what I was doing, I abused alcohol to anaesthetize myself. I was trying to numb my emotional and psychological pain from coping with the abuse that comes from having an alcoholic father. The hurt felt endless.

Later, when my first marriage was in crisis, I again turned to alcohol as a refuge, as a way of running away. What saved me? What stopped me spiralling down into becoming addicted? Meditation. I discovered it almost by chance soon after my marriage fell apart. Determined not to fall apart myself, I looked for a way of coping with the stress and came across meditation. Experiencing the power of mindfulness, I later trained to become a mindfulness teacher, qualifying in 2007, in the early days before mindfulness had really caught on.

Alcohol and mindfulness are two threads that have woven their way through my life. My answer to alcohol and the consequences of alcohol is mindfulness. My answer to suffering is mindfulness. I believe that whatever our suffering, mindfulness can help alleviate it. It enables me to be with emotional pain without needing to numb myself or self-medicate.

Just writing about this now dredges up the past. I take a break to work out how to comfort myself, how to bring compassion to myself and my painful memories. I make myself a hot drink. This simple gesture with the intention of being kind to myself is enough. For me mindfulness is all about self-compassion, self-nurture. This is what comes when I bring awareness to the present moment, to my experience now, especially in a moment of suffering.

Since 2007, I've taught many groups, including soldiers returning from Iraq and Afghanistan and National Health Service therapists. The power of mindfulness to turn people's lives around never ceases to amaze me. For that reason I'm delighted to have this opportunity to share with you what this ancient way of being has to offer us.

Mindfulness

In the same way that words can only point to ultimate reality, can only be a signpost, this book can only be a signpost to the breadth and depth of mindfulness. Mindfulness is above all a practice, a way of life, and it can only be learnt experientially. For that reason I've included mindfulness practices for you in Part 2 of the book. They will I hope whet your appetite for more, seeking out mindfulness courses, signing up for online trainings or downloading free audio recordings of practices.

On our journey towards healing it's worth remembering that mindfulness is only one of the skills, tools and support we need. It's not intended to replace but rather complement other resources such as self-help groups or psychotherapy.

Is this book for you?

- If you're in recovery and already abstinent, mindfulness offers a way of consolidating that, of taking your recovery deeper and further. It is also recognized as a powerful tool in relapse prevention, often an issue in the early days of recovery. Other issues may also be coming up. You may be getting in touch with underlying anxiety or pain, emerging anger and frustration or issues of panic or control. The approach in this book can help with these and any other overwhelming emotions.
- If your aim is to cut back or even to cut out drinking, mindfulness can help, with either moderating your intake or establishing abstinence.
- If you tend to think 'My drinking's not that bad', the very fact that you've picked this book up suggests it may well be for you.

- If your health is beginning to suffer and deep down you know it is because of your drinking, then this book is for you. Maybe you have a sense of not being able to get through the day, or even an evening, without a drink. If someone has suggested you should – I prefer could – 'get help', then this book will support you in that.
- If your work involves heavy social drinking with colleagues or clients that seems to be spiralling out of control, and especially if you work in the booze trade, then this book will help you explore that.
- If you've ever woken up deeply depressed, hangover or no hangover, feel life's not worth living without drink, or just feel generally low and down even though sober, this book shows how mindfulness can help. It can help you work through depression and stabilize feelings or moods that might threaten your sobriety, although you may need other assistance too, such as counselling or psychotherapy.
- If you feel your happiness lies in the hands of others (be that substances, friends, or lovers), the mindfulness practices in this book can encourage the self-sufficiency that is so important in dependency issues.
- If you've ever fallen down the stairs, drunk or hungover, or had another accident, or woken up with 'lost time' (i.e. a blackout) after drinking, this book is definitely for you (though do seek other help as well, such as from your doctor and/or support group).

- If you're falling down the stairs of your life, your partner has thrown you out or you've lost your job, this book can be the first step back up.

Why does mindfulness lend itself so well to recovery?

Mindfulness is so well suited for our journeys of recovery partly because it is a potent tool for self-management; we can use it as a self-help approach anywhere and anytime. But perhaps more importantly, it is because you can treat it as either a secular or spiritual practice. The choice is yours. The twelve-step approach of Alcoholics Anonymous (AA) is unquestionably spiritual, with its emphasis on a Higher Power, and has been hugely successful. Some consider spiritual transformation essential for lasting sobriety. Not everyone, however, wants to pursue this path. If this includes you, you can simply take the mindfulness practices in their own right and use them in a more secular way. They will still benefit you.

My stance is, however, mainly transpersonal, in other words spiritual. As Christina Grof, a recovering alcoholic and author of *The Thirst for Wholeness* says: 'The success of Alcoholics Anonymous (AA) and the many twelve-step fellowships that have modelled themselves after its program attests to the power and importance of the spiritual dimension in the understanding and treatment of addiction' (p. 19).

How does mindfulness help with recovery?

I've chosen to focus on three main ways mindfulness helps:

1 addressing our deeper longing;
2 cultivating self-compassion;
3 helping with relapse prevention.

You'll find a chapter on each in Part 1 of the book. Chapter 1, Craving or longing?, addresses the deeper, underlying longing that is masked by our physiological cravings for alcohol.

Increasingly those in recovery are sharing the spiritual dimension of their journeys to health and healing. As Christina Grof sees it, 'alcoholics and addicts are intense seekers who have made the mistake of looking for answers in the wrong place'.

The second way mindfulness assists with recovery, in Chapter 2, From self-harm to self-care, is by helping us cultivate self-compassion. Of the various qualities we cultivate through mindfulness, the most crucial for our recovery is self-compassion. If we're to begin to cope with the feelings drinking is masking or numbing, we need this. Whether it's loneliness or shame or feelings of alienation or inadequacy, we can only begin to cope without our anaesthetic if we learn to cultivate self-compassion.

We're aiming to let go of self-blame, self-criticism and self-loathing and move towards self-nurture and self-care. So we look at why compassion must be a central component of a mindfulness-based approach; why recovery without compassion simply doesn't make sense.

In this second chapter we'll also look at other qualities mindfulness helps us to cultivate and we'll explore the principles of how this approach works, starting with moment-by-moment awareness. What does it mean to live in the present moment? What does that feel like? Where twelve-step programmes encourage you to take one day at a time, the beauty of mindfulness is that we need only take one *moment* at a time. That's all we need to get through. Another principle we'll explore is the notion of being with, even stepping towards, what is painful and challenging. In other words, in Chapter 2 we'll look at what mindfulness is and how it works.

In Chapter 3 we look at another vital aspect of the recovery process, 'Staying on track'. This is the third way mindfulness specifically assists recovery; it has been shown to be particularly helpful with preventing relapse. We look at the role of stress as a major trigger of relapse and how mindfulness is the ultimate stress buster, helping us identify our own personal triggers and stressors. We also draw on the research evidence and clinical practice of valuable programmes such as Mindfulness-Based Addiction Recovery (MBAR), developed by the Addictive Behaviors Research Centre at the University of Washington. Similar mindfulness courses to help with recovery are being delivered in the UK, for instance by

Breathing Space in London and Action on Addiction in Salisbury.

Part 2 covers the mindfulness practices. I highly recommend you download free audio recordings of some of the practices. Use these alongside the text, especially when doing the all-important Body Scan. There is a free version available through my website: <www.catherine-g-lucas.com>. You'll find other details under 'Useful addresses and resources' at the end of the book.

By practising, you'll grasp experientially all the amazing benefits of mindfulness. My hope is that you'll integrate it into your life! The fundamental teaching of mindfulness is that we don't need to suffer; nobody needs to suffer. The more mindful we can be, the more aware and awake we can be, the more we can let go of our distress and the mental causes of it. As Achaan Chah, the founder of the Thai Forest Tradition, writes in *A Still Forest Pool*:

> If you let go a little, you will have a little peace. If you let go a lot, you will have a lot of peace. If you let go completely, you will know complete peace and freedom. Your struggles with the world will have come to an end. (p. 73)

Part 1

How does mindfulness help?

1

Craving or longing?

> *There was a deep yearning within me to connect with something more.*
>
> Richard

Alcohol, and its abuse, is so embedded in our culture that its grip is silent. It goes unseen, unnoticed. Yet always, always, the drinking masks something else going on under the surface. The drinking is not the real issue, not the real problem, though it does a very good job of pretending to be.

Using alcohol, or self-harming in any other way, is a coping mechanism. It's a way of coping with underlying wounding, trauma or abuse, a way of numbing ourselves to our emotional pain. The challenge is that often this coping strategy creates such chaos and drama in our lives that the drinking soon becomes the 'problem'. We, along with those around us, can lose sight of the underlying psychological or mental health issues.

If our consumption is not quite as out of control, we face a different challenge: our drinking is so socially acceptable that we don't even realize or acknowledge a problem, that there's an underlying issue we're not coping with. Here is Richard's experience with denial. We'll hear more of his story later.

Richard's story

A friend took me to my first AA Twelve Steps meeting. I knew she was part of the Fellowship – as it is called – but I was in sufficient denial that I thought I was going there to support her. The truth of the matter was that she had discerned that I too was alcoholic and could not stop drinking through my unaided will.

I had known that there was something wrong as my consumption ramped up past what even I could consider normal drinking. But knowing about it, and doing something, are light years apart. Besides, I appeared to function quite well. I had a successful marriage, a promising career, and had tamed 14 acres of wilderness to build a homestead for my new family. But the art of deception is second nature to many alcoholics; starting with self-deception at the root. After all, I rationalized, I wasn't on the hard stuff, didn't drink (most days) until after work ended, and nobody was complaining about my behaviour. Yet.

It somehow eluded me that my cellar of home-brewed wine had reached the epic proportions of a small estate winery – a friend counted over 5,000 bottles. My rationale was that I had to have enough left over from my personal consumption so that there would be sufficient quantities that would have a vintage of more than a few weeks. In fact I started my own vineyard to ensure a constant supply. My batches were in the hundreds of gallons. Such is the justification and rationale of the alcoholic mind.

As Dr Gabor Maté, an expert in the field, says, how much or how often is not that relevant. Some dismiss their addictive tendencies, saying, for example, 'I can't be an alcoholic. I don't drink that much' or 'I only drink at certain times.' The issue, Maté affirms, is not the amount or the frequency, but the impact.

Why the pain?

Dr Maté works in downtown Vancouver with some of the most wounded, traumatized and abused people who become addicts. His raw account of their lives, of the trajectories that lead them into using drugs and alcohol, makes the underlying emotional, psychological and mental health issues stark and clear. He is quick to point out the 'uniformly tragic past' of his patients, with 'childhood experiences almost too sordid to believe'. Like the father who 'drilled into his twin sons the notion that they were nothing but pieces of s**t'. One committed suicide as a teenager, the other became a lifelong addict. Hard-core abuse invariably leads to hard-core substance abuse. At the extreme end of the spectrum, his work helps us to understand the underlying causes, which may be more masked, more difficult to discern in addiction that seems less severe.

Maté has struggled with addiction himself; his expertise in the field is founded on both his personal and professional experiences. 'Addictions always originate in pain, whether felt openly or hidden in the unconscious', he writes in his book *In the Realm of Hungry Ghosts*.

> Not all addictions are rooted in abuse or trauma, but I do believe they can all be traced to painful experience. A hurt is at the centre of *all* addictive behaviours . . . The wound may not be as deep and the ache not as excruciating, and it may even be entirely hidden – but it's there. (p. 44)

The research confirms this. The Adverse Childhood Experiences (ACE) Study investigated, in thousands of people, ten different types of painful experience, including parental divorce, family violence, death of a parent, drug or alcohol abuse in the family and physical or sexual abuse. The study found that there is a two- to threefold increase in the likelihood of early alcohol abuse for every emotionally traumatic experience in childhood. 'Overall, these studies provide evidence that stress and trauma are common factors associated with consumption of alcohol at an early age as a means to self-regulate negative or painful emotions', the researchers reported (S. R. Dube et al., quoted in Maté, p. 199).

In another study of over 17,000 middle-class Americans, Dr Vincent Felitti, the chief investigator, found '[t]he basic cause of addiction is predominantly experience-dependent during childhood' (quoted in Maté, p. 187). At a personal level, these studies make sense when I think of my alcoholic father. He was born at the very beginning of the Second World War and his own father died when he was two. Stress and trauma set in early for my father. The same was true for Richard.

Richard's story

I was one of the supposedly privileged children whose parents sent us away to boarding school. I spent 60 per cent of my youth in the hands of those who were attracted to employment where they could mete out punishment and abuse to vulnerable young boys. To say these institutions were barbaric may be overstating the case. However, it isn't too difficult to understand that wrenching a child of eight to be exposed to a culture of punishment, bullying and lack of love or real care can leave some deep scars.

As the comedian Russell Brand, who has been clean and sober for over a decade, puts it, 'The reason I became a drug addict was because it was too painful not to.' This drive to numb ourselves is powerful. Using substances as an emotional anaesthetic is a recurring theme that Dr Maté sees with his clients. It is their 'attempt to escape distress': 'The question is never "Why the addiction?" but "Why the pain?"' (pp. 35, 36).

The deeper pain

There is another pain that runs deeper than emotional pain. Beyond our psychological suffering there is another driver that runs much more subconsciously and pushes us to seek refuge in our addictions. It has resulted in 'our addiction to a way of life that has been intoxicating us all', to quote Brand again.

Why, as a society, are we pursuing a level of consumerism that is destroying our planet, our source of food and life, stripping the earth of her natural resources faster than she can possibly replenish herself? And why is 'much of our culture', to cite Maté, 'geared towards enticing us away from ourselves, into externally directed activity'? He tells us:

> A sense of deficient emptiness pervades our entire culture . . . [the] addict is more painfully conscious of this void than most people . . . The rest of us find other ways of suppressing our fear of emptiness or of distracting ourselves from it. (p. 45)

Christina Grof, in *The Thirst for Wholeness*, seems to confirm this when she tells us that 'many recovering addicts and alcoholics report that once the physical craving for the drug is eliminated, a deeper craving still remains'. In her view:

> This intense and at times painful craving is deep thirst for our own wholeness, our spiritual identity . . . I believe that this fervent thirst for wholeness, as well as the discomfort with it, is the underlying impulse behind addictions. This deep yearning goes beyond the very real physiological craving of those of us who become hooked into the cycle of chemical addiction. (pp. 15–18)

Grof writes about this deeper drive, this deeper longing. In our disconnected, ego-driven world it is a longing for connection, a longing for meaning, a longing to feel part of the whole and to feel whole.

We can see this, as Carl Jung did when advising the founders of Alcoholics Anonymous, as a spiritual longing. To help fill this emptiness, this thirst for connection with ourselves and with something greater than ourselves, Jung encouraged 'the development of spirituality as an antidote to alcoholism'. Specifically, he advocated 'a vital spiritual experience' as the one thing that could really help someone in the grip of alcoholism.

It was just such a profound spiritual experience that enabled Bill Wilson, co-founder of AA, to stop drinking. Described in the book *Pass It On* and told by Grof, this is the story of Wilson, then a New York stockbroker.

Bill Wilson's story

As he sat in his hospital bed, once again under treatment for severe alcoholism, he desperately prayed to an unknown God to help him. Suddenly, he felt surrounded by white light and infused with mystical ecstasy, strength, and peace. 'I became acutely conscious of a Presence which seemed like a veritable sea of living spirit,' he wrote. 'I lay on the shores of a new world. "This," I thought, "must be the great reality. The God of the preachers."' (p. 32)

This 'vital spiritual experience' was so meaningful and profound for Wilson that he was able to stop drinking and, through the AA Fellowship he co-founded, help countless others do the same.

Acknowledging the spiritual level

Addiction affects us at every level, from the physical and emotional to the social *and* spiritual. As Grof explains:

> Those who have the insight that they are also dealing with a deep spiritual craving say that this divine discontent exists under and around all the other elements. Even as they acknowledge and deal with the other aspects of their addiction, if they do not directly address the spiritual craving, they are not adequately confronting their dilemma. (p. 19)

Richard's experience testifies to this. Here we pick up his story again.

Richard's story

Some instinct told me that there was a better way to live. From an early age I intuitively knew that there were inexplicable mysteries that held the key to a world beyond. Spiritual was a word yet to enter my vocabulary, but there was a deep yearning within me to connect with something more. I just didn't know how to access it.

I was driven to AA when I finally hit an utterly devastating rock bottom, where I had lost just about everything except my job (and barely able to keep that). If asked what my career choice was, I never would have said: 'I think I will become an alcoholic.' It is akin to ego annihilation when such an admission of total defeat comes. It's well known in most profound spiritual traditions that real transformation can only come from such a place of despair. This was not welcome news to me.

For many years I wasn't desperate enough – I hadn't lost everything – yet. Alcoholism is a progressive disease. It is relentlessly destructive. I have heard stories of people with one foot in the gutter, homeless, sucking rubbing alcohol from a brown paper bag, assuring everyone who would listen that it wasn't so bad, they could kick it, it was just a phase they were going through. For me it was the perfect medication to quell a gnawing internal pain that I was empty; I had a hole in my soul. That's what AA describes as a 'spiritual malady'.

The 'vital spiritual experience' that Carl Jung identified is what fills that void. When I am filled with Spirit – or what I call The Great Mystery – I need nothing more. It alone fills me to the brim. I am complete, not empty; connected, not alone. That for me is The Path: Finding my way Home.

In Christina Grof's experience:

> [W]ith support from the community of other recovering people, [individuals] begin to move toward a spiritual way of being. The emptiness slowly fills; the yearning gradually subsides. Over time, they develop a life infused with happiness, peace and compassion. (p. 20)

Why mindfulness?

How can mindfulness help us move towards this way of being? We find a clue in Dr Maté's *In the Realm of Hungry Ghosts*: 'The aching emptiness is perpetual because the substances, objects or pursuits we hope will soothe it are not what we really need . . . We haunt our lives without being fully present' (p. 1).

The key here is 'without being fully present'. This is what mindfulness can bring us, an ability to be present, to be here, now, without needing to distract ourselves, without needing to suppress anything. With mindfulness practice, we gradually become more present with ourselves, more in touch with our inner essence, our inner resources. On a personal note, Maté says he has found that ultimately what his patients care about is his, Maté's, 'presence or absence as a human being':

> What I have found is that when I do practice meditation, I find more ease in my life. I'm calmer, more emotionally present, more compassionate to others and far less reactive to external triggers. In other words, I'm more of a self-regulating adult and less prone to self-soothing, addictive behaviours. (p. 372)

Let's turn now to exploring mindfulness more fully. How does it work and how does it help? In the next chapter we'll look at the key principles of mindfulness. We'll also look at the main qualities we're developing as we practise, especially the all-important quality of self-compassion.

2

From self-harm to self-care

Mindfulness is a truly healing balm that can help put an end to our sense of alienation and help us heal both ourselves and our planet.

Thich Nhat Hanh

Despite the damaging effects for the environment of our 'intoxication' with consumerism and materialism, we seem powerless to stop ourselves. We seem powerless to consider the long-term consequences of our actions, unable to give up our dependence, in this case on things like cars and flying abroad. In response, Thich Nhat Hanh has written his moving *Love Letter to the Earth*. His answer is mindfulness. Whether the dependence in question is destroying our planet or destroying our health and relationships, whether the dependence is oil or alcohol, mindfulness can help us turn that around. Here is Ben's story of how he did just that, of how he went from self-harm to self-care.

Ben's story

I was first introduced to mindfulness and meditation through a course at the London Buddhist Centre for addiction recovery.

At that time, I was having difficulty in staying sober and I would nearly always have to play loud music in order to distract myself from my thoughts or to drown them out. However, I would notice immediately after the classes that I was feeling a sense of calmness. On my drive home, I wouldn't have to play music like I usually did – I could actually appreciate the silence. When I got home I would also be able to have a meal without having the TV on.

Engaging in regular exercise played a very important part in my recovery. I had found something I enjoyed, which was hindered by use of drugs and alcohol and was therefore incompatible past a certain level.

However, I would still experience episodes of anxiety and depression, which would sometimes lead to me relapsing. I eventually reached a turning point where I was fed up of being unhappy and fed up of always giving myself a hard time. I decided I would have to completely change my life rather than just trying to fix my addiction.

The most important change I made was to start a daily meditation practice, applying the same ethic to meditating that I'd applied in exercise (since fitness only improves with consistency, I realized it would be the same with the mind).

After more time practising mindfulness and meditation as well as discovering mindfulness talks on YouTube such as those by Eckhart Tolle, there was a much more noticeable shift in my consciousness. I found myself noticing beautiful details in nature and being able to appreciate things I probably would have overlooked previously. My memory improved quite a lot, as there was now less of my energy being expended on unhelpful anxious thinking. Pleasant memories from earlier life had the space to pop into my mind seemingly at random.

I also became more focused and creative with my work. The more I experienced these positive changes in my state of mind – the less I felt the urge to become intoxicated. In fact, I was no longer able to enjoy intoxication. Using drugs and alcohol began to feel deeply at odds and going completely in the wrong direction to the much more pleasant and calm state of mind that I had been tasting.

How mindfulness helps our recovery

Ben mentions he decided to completely change his life. Gradually he came to a place where to use drugs or alcohol would feel 'deeply at odds' with his new way of being in the world. When we embrace mindfulness fully it becomes a way of life for us, not simply a sticking plaster or yet another self-help tool.

There are many ways mindfulness helps on our journey towards healing. The three main aspects I've chosen to focus on are:

1 addressing our deeper longing;
2 cultivating self-compassion;
3 helping with relapse prevention.

In Chapter 1 we looked at the first of these, how mindfulness can be a response to our deeper longing for belonging, connection and wholeness. In this chapter we'll explore the principles and qualities of mindfulness. We'll see in particular how, through cultivating self-compassion, mindfulness helps us cope with any unbearable feelings, such as guilt or shame. Then, in Chapter 3, we'll look at how it can help us moderate or even stop drinking and prevent relapse.

What is mindfulness?

Mindfulness is a natural medicine, a 'healing balm' for the mind, a way of looking after ourselves, of taking care of ourselves with compassion. It is a way of answering that aching chasm within us, a way of healing any emptiness, shame or self-loathing. Above all it is an act of awakening; an act of awakening to the realization that we can no longer continue on our trajectory of self-destruction.

This notion of mindfulness as an act of awakening comes from Thich Nhat Hanh, in *Love Letter to the Earth*. Of all the variations in defining mindfulness, his is one of my favourites:

> Mindfulness is a nonjudgmental awareness of all that is happening inside us and around us. It takes us back to the foundation of happiness, which is being present in the here and now. Mindfulness is always mindfulness of something. We can be mindful of our breath, our footsteps, our thoughts, and our actions. Mindfulness requires that we bring all our attention to whatever we're doing, whether walking, breathing, brushing our teeth, or eating a snack. (p. 34)

When bringing 'all our attention to whatever we're doing' we can also think in terms of this simple equation:

> Mindfulness = intention + attention

Interestingly, science is now showing why and how the 'intention plus attention' of mindfulness can help those struggling with addiction. Studies into the effects of the conscious mental effort involved in mindfulness, this intention plus attention, show that the brain area activated is the pre-frontal cortex. This is the area that registers emotional self-regulation, the ability to self-soothe. Other research shows that it is precisely this emotional self-regulation that is damaged in addicts, often due to not receiving emotional nurturing as children.

One research conclusion is that the mental activity most critical to developing emotional self-regulation is therefore this ability to observe ourselves, our thoughts, feelings and behaviour, without judgement; in other words, mindfulness. The positive effects mindfulness practice has on our mental and emotional states can then be seen in the changing physiology of our brain circuits.

The principles of mindfulness

Moment-by-moment awareness

An 'awareness of all that is happening inside us' means noticing moment by moment three things: physical sensations in our body, our thoughts and our emotions. Through the practices you'll find in Part 2, we gradually cultivate this moment-by-moment awareness. As we do so, we become more aware of our tendencies, our habits. We become more aware of what triggers us; which emotions, what circumstances trigger us to 'need a drink'. By cultivating moment-by-moment awareness, we can start to see our patterns of behaviour.

By noticing physical sensations we're actually using all five senses – seeing, smelling, hearing, touching and tasting – to come into the now. This is our way into the present: moment-by-moment awareness of what is happening in the body. If we're totally focused on the piece of chocolate that is melting in our mouth, on our tongue, it's difficult to be thinking about anything else; neither the past nor the future exist in this moment. The sensations bring us right into the here and now. They anchor us in this moment.

The advantage of being present here and now is that more often than not it is our 'thinking' about the past or the future that gets us into trouble. That 'thinking' can be ruminating, dwelling, worrying, catastrophizing or obsessing, to name just a few. When we can drop all the stories about yesterday, last week or last year or tomorrow, next week or next year, and be here, now, it is extraordinarily liberating. It is, as Thich Nhat Hanh says, 'the foundation of happiness'.

Different kinds of suffering

One approach to suffering that my mindfulness students always find really helpful is to distinguish between primary suffering and secondary suffering. Vidyamala Burch, the founder of Breathworks and my mindfulness teacher, explains this very simply. The primary is suffering we have no control over; in my case, an alcoholic father who was emotionally and verbally abusive. The secondary is the suffering we cause to ourselves by resorting to damaging coping strategies. In my case, I later used alcohol as a way to numb the pain.

It's important to acknowledge that the primary suffering, whatever wounds, abuse or trauma we're carrying, is very real. We have no choice over that. The good news is that we do have a choice in how we respond to it. We may not be able to do anything to reduce the primary suffering but we can do a great deal to reduce the secondary. If someone is verbally abusive towards me and I feel distressed, most likely because my early wounding is being triggered, with mindful awareness I can choose to respond in a nurturing, healthy way. I could, for instance, talk it through with a trusted friend. If I reach for other more damaging ways of soothing myself, the consequences merely compound my pain.

The AA serenity prayer beautifully encapsulates this distinction between primary and secondary suffering. You can replace the word God with any term you feel more comfortable with:

> God grant me the serenity to accept the things I cannot change, the courage to change the things I can, and the wisdom to know the difference.

Being with the painful

A key principle of mindfulness involves being with, bearing with, what we find painful or challenging in some way. It means acknowledging the pain, the struggle, and opening to it, beginning to accept it, rather than trying to deny it or numb it out of existence.

It's a way of starting to be with ourselves and our suffering, bringing compassion to our pain, no longer running, hiding, resisting. When we run from our pain it chases us down the street. It can always run as fast, if not faster, than we can. In fact Achaan Chah, the Thai monk and teacher, says, 'To try to run away from our suffering is actually to run towards it.' What we need to do is turn and face it, even gently stepping towards it. This can be both challenging and powerful in recovery.

Dr Paramabandhu Groves is the director of Breathing Space, based at the London Buddhist Centre, delivering a range of mindfulness courses, including for recovery. A psychiatrist, he is also co-author of *Eight Step Recovery* with Valerie Mason-John. He said this to me about working with painful emotions:

> Many people in recovery struggle from negative mental states such as anger, anxiety and depression. These can be triggers that lead back into addictive behaviour or simply contribute to an individual's suffering. Mindfulness is a practical approach that gives people tools to work with difficult emotions.
>
> Firstly, mindfulness can help to bring awareness to these states of mind. Often people are not fully aware of their emotions, or only become aware of them when the emotions get very strong; they are then hard to work with or it is hard not to resort to addictive behaviour. Catching painful states of mind early on makes it far easier to head them off.
>
> Secondly, mindfulness can help to contain painful emotions. Even if they can't immediately be dissipated, mindfulness teaches ways to help stay with difficult mental states with acceptance, non-judgement and kindness. This allows them to be processed without acting from them in unhelpful ways.

Here is how Brendan describes being with, or bearing with, painful thoughts and emotions during his mindfulness practice. You can read more of his story in the next chapter.

Brendan's story

I suffered badly with unwanted painful thoughts and emotions and couldn't find relief. I had tried anti-depressants but they felt like a sticking plaster, i.e. just enough to stem the wound but doing nothing to heal it.

Some of the worst consequences of alcoholism ran on a loop through my mind while I sat with the monks . . .

At first I was exposed to the thoughts I was trying to avoid even more! To the extent that they were all I thought about. This was the exact opposite of what I actually wanted. What I came to realize was I could not escape them, but by sitting in the zazen [meditation] posture and being mindful of every thought and not engaging with any of it in any way, it 'burnt' itself out . . . the power of the thoughts diminished until they no longer crippled me with pain.

If we're even to begin to be able to do this kind of healing work, to reap the long-term benefits, if we're even to begin to be able to be with our painful emotions, our guilt, our shame, our self-blame, we need to cultivate compassion for ourselves. This is all part of learning mindfulness.

Cultivating compassion

If being with or stepping towards the painful helps so much, we can only hope to do that when we bring deep caring and kindness towards ourselves. Coping with shame and blame, self-hatred and self-criticism means cultivating compassion, compassion towards our own suffering. As Ben said, 'I eventually reached a turning point where I was fed up of being unhappy and fed up of always giving myself a hard time.'

Kristin Neff, a psychologist, researcher and the author of *Self Compassion*, identifies three key ingredients to self-compassion: self-kindness; recognition of our common humanity; mindfulness. She says:

> Self-kindness, by definition, means that we stop the constant self-judgement and disparaging internal commentary that most of us have come to see as normal. It requires us to *understand* our foibles and failures instead of condemning them. It entails clearly seeing the extent to which we harm ourselves through relentless self-criticism. (p. 42)

Those of us who come from wounded families and backgrounds of abuse are likely to have a louder and stronger inner voice cutting us down at every opportunity. Judging ourselves for judging ourselves is not the answer. Self-compassion, hand-in-hand with mindfulness, is.

Sensing our common humanity is important because it helps us cut through feelings of isolation and alienation. When we understand that everybody experiences fears and tears, that everybody wants to be free from suffering, that everybody fundamentally wants to be happy, then we no longer feel alone but part of something bigger than ourselves, bigger than little me. As Neff puts it:

> When we're in touch with our common humanity, we remember that feelings of inadequacy and disappointment are shared by all. This is what distinguishes self-compassion from self-pity. Whereas self-pity says 'poor me', self-compassion remembers that everyone suffers, and it offers comfort because everyone is human. The pain I feel in difficult times is the same pain that you feel in difficult times. (p. 62)

Loving Kindness practices are sometimes called Kindly Awareness (see Chapter 5). They help to foster this sense of common humanity. In the process of cultivating more gentleness and kindness towards ourselves, we automatically become more compassionate to those around us. If you remember from Chapter 1, this is precisely what Dr Gabor Maté says: '[W]hen I do practice meditation, I find more ease in my life. I'm calmer, more emotionally present, more compassionate to others.'

The key to unlocking self-compassion is Neff's third ingredient, mindfulness. It's only through the moment-by-moment awareness of our bodies, thoughts and emotions that we can notice when we're not being kind to ourselves or when there is suffering that needs soothing. As she says:

> when we improve our mindfulness skills, we automatically increase our ability to be self-compassionate. Several studies have demonstrated that participation in an eight-week MBSR (Mindfulness-Based Stress Reduction) course increases self-compassion levels. Similarly, studies have demonstrated that experienced mindfulness meditators have more self-compassion than those who are less experienced. (p. 101)

On a personal note

I've found Neff's work really helpful in getting me to notice when I'm suffering. 'This feels painful. What can I do right now to help?' or 'This is a moment of suffering. How can I be kind to myself?' are the sort of phrases I've started using. They have made a huge difference to me, knowing that there is always something I can do to ease my pain. Even if the answer is simply to make myself a cup of hot cocoa or get out for a walk, I have the sense of being kind to myself, which is so, so valuable.

Mindfulness and self-compassion go hand in hand. As we learn mindfulness so we also cultivate self-compassion. I remember one mindfulness student who always seemed to be exceptionally hard on himself, meting out harsh self-condemnation and self-judgement. All it took was for me gently to point out his tendency to him; his mindfulness practice did the rest. His attitude towards himself changed completely over the eight-week programme.

Another aspect of compassion is exploring our thoughts, emotions and behaviour with compassionate curiosity, a sort of compassionate self-enquiry. In his book *In the Realm of Hungry Ghosts*, Dr Maté writes:

> Posed in a tone of compassionate curiosity, 'Why?' is transformed from rigid accusation to an open-minded, even scientific question. Instead of hurling an accusatory brick at your own head (e.g. 'I'm so stupid; when will I ever learn?', etc.) . . . we adopt toward ourselves the attitude of the empathic friend, who simply wants to know what's going on with us . . . 'Hmm. I wonder what drove me to do this again?' (p. 337)

Responding rather than reacting

Our final principle, something that mindfulness enables us to do, is to respond rather than react, in ways that are helpful rather than harmful. Reaching for a drink is the habitual reaction; finding other less destructive ways of soothing ourselves is responding.

By learning moment-by-moment awareness and gradually increasing our self-awareness, we gain space around our tendencies, our emotional and thought patterns. We notice just that little bit earlier that we've been triggered and are experiencing craving, both important issues that we'll look at in the next chapter. We buy enough time to be able to have choice. Rather than reacting in a knee-jerk, damaging way, we're gradually able to respond in a more nurturing, healing way. We move away from self-harm towards self-care.

Your personal scale

Figure 1 shows an example of a self-care scale that you can copy into a notepad, to gauge how you're doing at any one time. Simply mark along it what you consider to be your level of self-harm or self-care. You could use it at regular times each day or after challenging situations have arisen or however works best for you.

In this chapter we've looked at what mindfulness is and how it works. We've discussed some of its key principles, including the all-important, counter-intuitive moving towards our pain. We can only do this when we develop self-compassion. Ultimately, if we want to move from self-harm to self-care, it is self-compassion that will enable us to do so. In her book *Self Compassion*, Kristin

We can do all the different activities in our lives in ways that range from self-harming to self-caring. On the spectrum below, mark how you think you're doing this week or this day. You might like to make a note beforehand of any stressful or challenging situation you've recently had to cope with, to help you assess how you responded.

Challenging situation..

....

....

Self-harming *Self-caring*

Eating ....

Sleeping ....

Studying/working ....

Exercising ....

Relaxing ....

Relationship ....

Friendships ....

Family ....

Alcohol ....

One other area of your choice...

....

Today's date ....

Figure 1 Example of a self-care scale

Neff writes: 'self-compassion involves valuing yourself in a deep way, making choices that lead to well-being in the long term. Self-compassion wants to heal dysfunctions, not perpetuate them' (p. 166).

As we turn our attention next to how mindfulness can help you moderate or stop drinking and prevent relapse, it's worth noting again Dr Gabor Maté's opinion:

> I don't propose meditation and mindfulness as panaceas. It is futile to dream of corralling a group of active . . . alcoholics into a meditation class. To pursue such practices one requires mental resources, a commitment to emotional clarity, an access to teaching and some mental space in one's life . . . But for people whose lives are blighted by addictions without being totally gripped by them, these practices can help light the way to wholeness. (p. 355)

3

Staying on track

Mindfulness is an integral part of my recovery for which I am eternally grateful.

Brendan

Only us

In recovery there is no them and us, only us. '[T]he drive to escape the moment is a common, nearly universal human characteristic', as Dr Gabor Maté puts it in *In the Realm of Hungry Ghosts*. It's just a question of degree. For the person struggling with addiction that drive 'is magnified to the point of desperation' (p. 356). When we acknowledge the extent to which we all seek escape from the present, the extent to which we all run away from ourselves, we can have an honest and compassionate conversation about addiction and recovery. We can see the addictive tendencies in each of us and know that we all have painful experiences and all want to be free from pain. We can appeal to the common humanity we share. A way of life rooted in mindfulness can help each and every one of us, no matter where we are along the spectrum.

Sustaining recovery

Here is Brendan's experience of how mindfulness has helped him establish and sustain his recovery.

Brendan's story

My name is Brendan and I'm a recovering alcoholic. What do I mean by alcoholic? I mean I have lost the ability to control my drinking alcohol once I *start* drinking. Once I start drinking I cannot predict when and where it will end. This has led to dire consequences, such as police cells, broken relationships, homelessness, loss of career and friendships. Worst of all was the impact on my family.

What do I mean by recovering? I mean that I don't drink at all because of the aforementioned reason and I am recovering from the consequences from when I did drink alcohol. For example repairing relationships, recovering career, etc. The most long-lasting consequence for me is the physical, emotional and mental fact that if I drink alcohol I don't know what the outcome will be, and it could be really bad. Why is this a problem? Because we live in a stressful society and very demanding culture that traditionally manages stress by using alcohol. I have had to learn how to live a normal life surrounded by alcohol while not using alcohol. I have used many methods over the years to help me in my recovery. One of them is mindfulness.

My experience of mindfulness practice can best be described as Soto Zen meditation. I first came across this practice many years ago synchronistically as a result of searching for release from the mental and emotional anguish I was experiencing. I was directed to Throstle Hole Buddhist Monastery near Hexham in Northumberland. I always remember standing in front of the altar and being rooted to the ground by a feeling of intense energy going through me. I interpreted this as a sign that I should stay and learn more.

At this time in my life, even though I had stopped drinking, I was suffering badly with the consequences of being brought up in an alcoholic family and my own maladaptation as an alcoholic. I suffered badly with unwanted painful thoughts and emotions and couldn't find relief. I had tried anti-depressants but they felt like a sticking plaster, i.e. just enough to stem the wound but doing nothing to heal it.

In the monastery the monks taught me zazen, which can be summarized in one sentence as 'sitting with no deliberate thought'. This was exactly what I was looking for as I felt I was being punished by myself as well as my past. It took a lot of practice sitting with the monks on weekends and retreats in freezing cold halls for many weeks just to get an insight into the experience of zazen. At first I was exposed to the thoughts I was trying to avoid even more! To the extent that they were all I thought about. This was the exact opposite of what I actually wanted. What I came to realize was I could not escape them, but by sitting in the zazen posture and being mindful of every thought and not engaging with any of it in any way, it 'burnt' itself out.

Some of the worst consequences of alcoholism ran on a loop through my mind while I sat with the monks. Without their discipline keeping me grounded I doubt I would have made it through, but eventually I did and the power of the thoughts diminished until they no longer crippled me with pain.

I still practise mindfulness but the context and emphasis has changed. What I mean is that even though the practice is still the same, i.e. sitting with no deliberate thought, I now practise it in my home, in the car, at work, etc. It is a transformative tool that travels with me. My goal is to live in mindfulness. It's rare I achieve this. What happens is I drift in and out. I still don't drink alcohol, because I will always be an alcoholic, that is once I start drinking I can't predict the consequences but my best guess would be that it will be bad.

Mindfulness is an integral part of my recovery for which I am eternally grateful, as well as to the monks of Throstle Hole for showing me the way.

Brendan is one of a growing number of recovering alcoholics who use mindfulness to help keep them on track. As he rightly points out, stress is a huge issue in our lives today. As Gabor Maté notes, there has never before, during peacetime, been a generation that is so stressed. Brendan also mentions how widespread the use of alcohol is in an attempt to cope with that stress.

Stress: a double whammy

Research in the addiction field confirms Brendan's impressions: one of the main triggers of self-harming with alcohol is stress. Put very simply, stress plays a dual role in our alcohol abuse. It makes us more likely to turn to alcohol in the first place *and* more likely to relapse when we have managed a period of abstinence.

Dr Maté has studied the research literature and conducted his own interviews. Early trauma, abuse or wounding, he says, impacts on how human beings respond to stress throughout their lives, and stress goes hand in hand with addiction. Stress is the physiological response of an organism when it meets excessive demands on its coping mechanisms, either biological or psychological.

Perhaps not surprisingly, for humans, according to Hans Selye, a stress researcher, 'the most important stressors are emotional' (quoted in Maté, p. 202). This ties in with what Alan Marlatt, Director of the Addictive Behaviors Research Center at the University of Washington, found in his relapse prevention research: strong negative emotional states, such as anger, anxiety and depression, are all potential triggers for relapse, triggering the need to 'self-medicate'.

Burying our pain

Many of us don't realize we're carrying any emotional wounding or that we're vulnerable to stress. As a child growing up in an alcoholic family, that was the norm for me. I didn't realize my father's behaviour was verbally and emotionally 'abusive'. Even more pertinent is the way many of us bury our wounds as a self-protective mechanism. We forget or even deny severe emotional pain.

This is highlighted by a study reported in the *Journal of Consulting and Clinical Psychology* following up on young girls who had been treated for proven sexual abuse on an emergency ward. Contacted 17 years later as adults, 40 per cent of these abused women either did not remember or even completely denied the event. Yet their memory was found to be sound for other episodes in their lives.

This repression of painful emotions and events has the effect of dulling us overall emotionally. We can't be selective; everything gets subdued. I remember one of my mindfulness students whose baby had been born with special needs. As she struggled to cope with her child's needs, and the stress and prejudice she encountered from other mothers, she shut down emotionally. She went through her days feeling numb. Her pain was blunted but so too was her capacity to experience happiness, let alone joy. The mindfulness course enabled her to begin to feel again, to feel safe enough to start opening back up to all her emotions.

Not realizing we're carrying wounding, or not consciously remembering it but needing to protect and insulate ourselves from it, has unfortunate consequences. It means that many struggling with forms of self-harm don't see the link between their self-harming and their early experiences. Yet understanding that link is crucial to our healing process, crucial to our recovery. Without that understanding, we're more than likely to think that the drinking is the problem, when in fact it is a coping mechanism for what needs attending to underneath. As I mentioned at the very beginning, alcohol does a very good job of pretending to be the 'problem'. We need insight and understanding into ourselves and our patterns of behaviour not to be hoodwinked. Mindfulness helps us gain that.

We also need to understand the roots of our drinking if we're to begin to cultivate the self-compassion we've already talked about. The alternative is that we blame ourselves. In recovery, it is not about blaming anyone.

To return to how early wounding impacts on how we respond to stress all our lives, Dr Maté tells us in *In the Realm of Hungry Ghosts*: 'Early stress establishes a lower "set point" for a child's internal stress system: such a person becomes stressed more easily than normal throughout her life' (p. 202). Maté quotes Dr Bruce Perry, Senior Fellow at the Child Trauma Academy in Houston, Texas:

> A child who is stressed early in life . . . is triggered more easily, is more anxious and distressed. Now, compare a person – child, adolescent or adult – whose baseline arousal is normal with another whose baseline state of arousal is at a higher level. Give them both alcohol: both may experience the same intoxicating effect, but the one who has this higher physiological arousal will have the added effect of feeling pleasure from the relief of that stress. (p. 202)

Mindfulness for staying on track

Given that stress can make alcoholics of us in the first place *and* increase our vulnerability to relapse, stress management techniques are vital. The good news is that mindfulness is a stress management tool par excellence. In our recovery, such an approach gives us the perfect tool to help cope with anything that might threaten our sobriety.

Jon Kabat-Zinn pioneered the use of mindfulness in the field of health with the mindfulness-based stress reduction programme he created and the centre he set up at the University of Massachusetts Medical School. He and others have gathered the research evidence, including positive outcomes on blood pressure and heart rate, which are both stress indicators. It was stress-related high blood pressure that led Alan Marlatt to try meditation in the first place. His doctor encouraged him to conduct his own personal research experiment, both meditating and measuring his blood pressure daily. 'To my delight, my diastolic blood pressure showed a significant drop after the first 2 weeks of daily practice', writes Marlatt in the Preface to *Mindfulness-Based Relapse Prevention for Addictive Behaviors* (p. xiii). This in turn led to his life-long personal and professional interest in meditation and mindfulness.

Mindfulness-Based Relapse Prevention (MBRP)

MBRP is an approach that brings together cognitive-behavioural relapse prevention with mindfulness. Alan Marlatt and his team at the Addictive Behaviors Research Center (University of Washington) spent many years developing and researching MBRP. Papers on various aspects of MBRP can be found in academic journals such as *Addictive Behaviors*, *Addiction Research and Theory* and *Psychology of Addictive Behaviors*.

Reflecting on that journey, Marlatt said:

> Clearly there was medical evidence supporting the benefits of meditation as a tension-reduction practice. Given that both ongoing addictive behavior and risk for relapse go up as tension and stress increase, both at the physiological and psychological levels, it seemed clear that meditation could be a helpful coping skill in addiction treatment. (p. xiii)

The primary goals of Mindfulness-Based Relapse Prevention, as outlined on MBRP's website (see 'Useful addresses and resources' for website address), are:

1 develop awareness of personal triggers and habitual reactions, and learn ways to create a pause in this seemingly automatic process;
2 change our relationship to discomfort, learning to recognize challenging emotional and physical experiences and respond to them in skilful ways;
3 foster a nonjudgmental, compassionate approach towards ourselves and our experiences;

4 build a lifestyle that supports both mindfulness practice and recovery.

It's worth noting, as the last goal suggests, that mindfulness practice needs to be ongoing in order to help us sustain recovery. We need to create a lifestyle that will support both, as indeed Brendan has when he says: 'I still practise mindfulness . . . It is a transformative tool that travels with me . . . Mindfulness is an integral part of my recovery.'

MBRP programmes are also sometimes known as Mindfulness-Based Addiction Recovery (MBAR). One of the main benefits of these various courses is that we can learn to explore, and cultivate acceptance of, craving and urges. We can become more aware of triggers and habitual reactions as well as learning practical skills to help us in situations where we are at high risk of relapsing. As Marlatt said, 'I realized that mindfulness meditation could be helpful for people with addictive behavior in terms of coping with urges and craving, whether they are pursuing a goal of moderation or abstinence' (p. xiv).

In the Preface to *Mindfulness-Based Relapse Prevention*, he writes:

> Buddhist psychology emphasizes acknowledging, feeling, and accepting discomfort when it arises, and understanding the experience intimately, rather than endlessly attempting to run away from it. This is a compassionate approach, emphasizing acceptance and openness rather than guilt, blame, and shame about one's behavior. Mindfulness also promotes awareness of the changing

> nature of things; our minds, bodies, and environments are in a constant state of change.
>
> For example, consider the smoker who cannot imagine going 45 minutes without a cigarette, but who doesn't realize that his or her seemingly overwhelming desires may attenuate if he or she can just ride them out. Mindfulness can provide a 'skilful means' of coping with urges and craving that involves observing them, without being wiped out or consumed by them. Even though the smoker may feel that the urge to smoke will increase unless he or she gives in and lights up a cigarette, the smoker's urges and cravings will change on their own if he or she gives them time to pass. (pp. viii–ix)

MBRP and MBAR courses include specific practices such as Urge Surfing and SOBER (Stop, Observe, Breathe, Expand, Respond) to help cope with craving and high-risk triggering situations. You can find these practices in Part 2 of the book and they are also available as free audio downloads on the MBRP website (see 'Useful addresses and resources').

MBRP programmes in the UK

Programmes developed along MBRP lines or similar are available in London, through Breathing Space, and also in East Knoyle, Salisbury, through Action on Addiction. Devin Ashwood leads Action on Addiction's mindfulness programmes. He commented on both his experience and that of his students on the MBRP course in an email to me:

> addictive behaviours regularly become a default response to uncomfortable feelings in an attempt to bring relief. While this

> strategy may be effective in the very short term, it has the effect of reinforcing the addictive behaviour . . . Mindfulness training is very challenging for people in early recovery as it asks the student to tolerate and turn towards these difficult feelings, which are often experienced as urges or cravings. However, because it is this crucial process that is addressed through mindfulness training, it has the potential to be vitally transformative in recovering from addictions.
>
> My experience of teaching Mindfulness-Based Relapse Prevention to clients in recovery has highlighted how this cutting-edge intervention directly addresses the internal drives that sustain problematic addictive behaviours. A lightbulb often switches on for clients who engage with the programme for a number of weeks as they see how practising mindfulness is of direct relevance to the reason they sought help. After this, committing to a regular mindfulness practice becomes a natural part of this stage of their recovery.

Action on Addiction also offer teacher training. There are a few other qualified MBRP trainers around the country, for instance in Dorset. Details can be found at the back of the book under 'Useful addresses and resources'. As mindfulness becomes more and more established as a powerful therapeutic tool for recovery, there will no doubt be more and more of these courses available around the country.

As we get ready to dive into the mindfulness practices themselves in Part 2, there are a couple of simple 'props' you'll need. You may want to procure them now, as well as any audio recordings, so that you're ready to get started. One of the first meditations calls for raspberries. Any other fruit that has a certain 'zing' to it is fine if you can't get hold of raspberries. Another exercise involves experimenting with a food you don't like or that you even actively dislike. You may need to go shopping! In terms of audio recordings, you'll need to at least download the practice called the Body Scan. There is a free version available through my website: <www.catherine-g-lucas.com>.

Enjoy!

Part 2

The mindfulness practices

Introduction to the practices

It's best to wear loose, comfy clothes for all the mindfulness practices. It's surprising how much anything at all tight around the waist or abdomen restricts our breathing.

As I mentioned at the end of Part 1, you'll need a few simple props for the introductory practices. You may have already gathered these: a few raspberries, preferably organic or home grown, and some food or a snack that you actively dislike. Have fun with these practices as you sample your first taste of mindfulness!

After those, the first full, classic practice is the Body Scan. You will definitely need to download the audio recording to listen to it. There is a free version available through my website: <www.catherine-g-lucas.com>. For details of other versions, see 'Useful addresses and resources' at the back of the book.

The Body Scan is usually done lying down, so you'll need a suitable, comfortable surface or bed. Use a pillow or cushion but make sure you don't have it too high. The neck needs to be in natural, comfortable alignment with the body. Use a blanket or throw because the body temperature drops as we relax during this practice.

The other practices are usually done sitting up, so you'll need an upright chair, such as a dining chair, or a meditation cushion or stool, if you prefer. If you're using a chair, depending how tall you are, you may find it comfortable to have something under your feet. You could use a yoga block, or something like a cushion would work. It's also helpful to have a cushion in your lap to really support the hands and arms well. You may want a blanket or shawl of some sort to wrap around you. The aim is to make ourselves as comfortable as we can. It's all part of the self-nurturing that we're cultivating. At the same time our upright posture can support an alert, yet relaxed mind. Don't get too hung up on the details though; as long as you're comfortable, that's what matters.

I recommend that you download free audio recordings of some of the other practices too. These can be very helpful to listen to and work with alongside Part 2 of the book. The Mindfulness-Based Relapse Prevention website has excellent resources, all freely available. Again, you can find details at the back of the book.

A word about language: we talk about 'practices' because that's precisely what we're doing, practising. Also we tend to talk about 'the body' rather than 'your body', as a way of helping to remind us to watch it dispassionately, without getting so caught up in 'me' and 'mine'. When we realize we are so much more than our bodies, that we are not our thoughts and feelings, that we don't have to believe every thought we have is true, that we don't have to act on every feeling, we are well on our way to freedom.

Have fun with these practices; hold them lightly. You don't have to try too hard or force anything; let them be what they will be.

4

A first taste of mindfulness

Be mindful . . . Then your mind will become still in any surroundings, like a clear forest pool.

Achaan Chah

Here I'm going to give you an initial flavour of what mindfulness is all about, in an experiential way. You will begin to get a sense of, and develop, some of our key mindfulness principles. The Raspberry Relish (yes, it involves eating raspberries . . .) is about starting to cultivate moment-by-moment awareness; the Noting practice, too. The kindness and hugging exercises help with beginning to build self-compassion, whereas Food, Not-So-Glorious Food is about an initial experience of being with, or even stepping towards, what is challenging or difficult in some way.

A few pointers

For most of these practices we sit quietly, eyes closed. This is to reduce the stimulus and distraction of seeing what is around us. It helps us focus more on what is going on inside moment by moment. If at first you don't feel so comfortable with closing your eyes, you can simply soften your gaze and look down towards the floor in front of you. Make sure your phone is turned off so you won't be disturbed or interrupted.

Raspberry Relish

You'll need a few fresh raspberries for this practice. The point of this exercise is to start noticing sensations in more detail, to explore something more closely than before. It is through noticing and exploring physical sensations that we find our way into the present moment, through the body. The flavour of the raspberry is right here, right now, not two hours ago or in two hours' time. The body is here with us, always present in this way. Any physical sensations are in *this* moment. This is our way into the present moment. This is our ticket to 'now'.

The practice

As with all these practices, settle down making sure you won't be interrupted, turning your phone off, for instance. Sit quietly for a few minutes, just looking at the raspberry, exploring its colour, its shape and honeycombed structure, those furry little hairs on its surface, whatever you see.

Taking your time, when you're ready, put it in your mouth without chewing or sucking it. Hold it there, feeling the texture against your tongue. Notice as much about that as possible. Can you feel the slightly furry surface, the tiny hairs? Can you feel the individual segments of the honeycomb? Notice how the raspberry has little or no flavour yet. What's it like to resist immediately biting into it?

Again, taking your time, when you're ready, slowly push the raspberry against your tongue so that it almost melts. Can you still feel the individual seeds or segments as it starts to break up? How would you describe the flavour? Does that linger after you've swallowed it?

Notice how, while doing this practice, you're totally absorbed in the present moment, you're totally focused on the sensory experience right here, right now. If you become aware of the mind wandering off, that's perfectly normal; simply bring it back gently to the sensations.

If you would like to, you can explore further with two or three more raspberries.

Take the time to reflect on what you noticed or learnt with this exercise. It represents the foundation of mindful eating that we will cover later, in Chapter 7, 'Everyday mindfulness'.

Noting

Noting practice involves taking mental notes rather than written ones. It's very helpful for mindfulness throughout the day as it lends itself to any situation. We simply note mentally whatever is arising in the mind. By noting it, we become more consciously aware of it. So, for example, if I note that I'm feeling rejected, I become more consciously aware of feeling rejected. If I note that my feet are cold, I become more aware of having cold feet. This awareness then gives me the choice to do something about it, to respond appropriately, by sharing my feelings with the other person, or putting some socks on, for instance.

We can also take note of the breath. Breathing is something the body does so automatically much of the time we're hardly even aware of it. Thich Nhat Hanh offers these simple phrases we can use at any time of day:

> Breathing in, I know I'm breathing in.
> Breathing out, I know I'm breathing out.

The practice

Sit quietly, eyes closed for about ten minutes. Make a mental note of whatever comes to mind, any thoughts or emotions, any physical sensations, any sounds you might hear, and so on. Your noting might go something like this: 'dog barking', 'back aching', 'forgot to turn phone off', 'wondering what to have for lunch'. Every time something new comes into your awareness, simply label it, let it go and allow the mind to settle on the next experience.

If you haven't meditated before you may well be amazed at how busy and chatty the mind is, jumping from one thing to the next. The mind supposedly 'at rest' is far from it! You may also suddenly notice you've been daydreaming for the last few minutes, caught up in a particular train of thought, completely forgetting about noting. That's fine; simply note 'daydreaming' and come back to the practice. Every time we notice the mind has wandered off is actually a moment of mindfulness.

This Noting practice is a very good introductory one for helping us become more aware of what's happening moment by moment, giving us more choice in how we respond, making us more likely to choose a self-caring option than a self-harming one. You can use it at any point during the day. The more you do, the more mindful your day will be.

Kindness practices

Compassion, especially towards ourselves first and foremost, is central to mindfulness. Here are some brief introductory practices; some initial, simple explorations of the tender power of kindness.

Kindness reflection

This is from *Eight Step Recovery* by Valerie Mason-John and Dr Paramabandhu Groves (p. 99).

The practice

Give yourself five minutes. Settle your body into a comfortable posture. If you are sitting, allow your body to come into an upright posture without forcing or straining. If you are lying down, become aware of your spine. Take one or two deep breaths, exhaling slowly. Say to yourself gently and slowly the word 'kindness'. Notice any effects in your body, any images that come to mind, or any thoughts or feelings that appear. As best you can, be interested in any responses, whether pleasant or unpleasant. If there is no response that is completely fine too.

As with all these practices, you might like to journal about how that was for you, recording and exploring further any thoughts, feelings or inspirations. Journaling is a powerful tool on our journey to well-being and I recommend it highly. It can help you chart both your mindfulness and recovery paths. (See Philip Cowell, *Keeping a Journal*.)

More kindness practices

Here are some more ideas for touching into this all-important quality of self-compassion. Again, I've adapted these from Mason-John and Groves (pp. 109–10). Experiment with them to see what works best for you or try combining different ones together.

The practices

Sit quietly, maybe lighting a candle to help you settle and focus.

- ♥ Imagine your heart as a flower opening up, or use another image that evokes loving kindness for you.
- ♥ Put your hand on your heart and breathe into your heart, feeling your chest rising and falling.
- ♥ Imagine moving kindness around your whole body, or filling your whole body with kindness.
- ♥ Say a phrase to yourself, wishing yourself kindness, such as 'May I be well' or 'May I be happy' or 'May I be free from suffering.' Imagine that each phrase is like a tiny pebble and your body is like a pool or lake. As you say each phrase, imagine the pebble

dropping into your body and kindness rippling throughout your body.

- Imagine giving yourself a warm, tender hug.

A Selfie Hug

Let's take the last suggestion of imagining hugging yourself a bit further with this practice recommended by Kristin Neff in her book *Self Compassion*. She explains that when we actively soothe our own pain we are tapping into the care-giving system of mammals. One important way this system works is that it triggers the release of a hormone called oxytocin. Because of its role, it has become known as the hormone of love and bonding. By way of introduction to the practice she says:

> One easy way to soothe and comfort yourself when you're feeling badly is to give yourself a gentle hug. It seems a bit silly at first, but your body doesn't know that. It just responds to the physical gesture of warmth and care . . . Our skin is an incredibly sensitive organ. Research indicates that physical touch releases oxytocin, provides a sense of security, soothes distressing emotions, and calms cardiovascular stress. (p. 49)

The practice

If you notice that you're feeling tense, upset, sad, or self-critical, try giving yourself a warm hug, tenderly stroking your arm or face, or gently rocking your body. What's important is that you make a clear gesture that conveys feelings of love, care, and tenderness. If other people are around, you can often

> fold your arms in a non-obvious way, gently squeezing yourself in a comforting manner.
>
> Notice how your body feels after receiving the hug. Does it feel warmer, softer, calmer? It's amazing how easy it is to tap into the oxytocin system. (p. 50)

Aim to hug yourself at least three times a day for a week or two. Once you've got into it, it will be that much easier to give yourself a hug in difficult times, when you most need it. My sense, from my experience with the hug, is that skin-to-skin contact feels even more lovely. I suspect that it releases more oxytocin still. See what you think!

If at first you notice some resistance here, or to any of the kindness practices, you could journal about it. What is the resistance to do with? What's underneath it? Where's it coming from? If it's bringing up painful or sad emotions, take your time, be kind and gentle with yourself. We can step towards our pain as slowly and as gently as we need to, so as not to get overwhelmed by it. Take a break, nurture yourself and come back to the practice later when you feel more resourced.

Food, Not-So-Glorious Food

This starts to explore uncomfortable or painful experiences and helps us to work with them. We begin to see how mindfulness helps transform our relationship to such experiences. Because it is experiential, we start to get a feel for what it's like to stay with the discomfort, to bear with it. This is that counter-intuitive stepping towards what is painful or difficult, rather than resisting it, pushing it away. Treat this more as an experiment, as your personal psychological laboratory, keeping an open, curious mind. Remember the compassionate curiosity we discussed earlier.

The practice

The idea is to explore, in a way that feels manageable, what it's like to be with the difficult or challenging; in this case, the unpleasant. You're going to choose a food that you strongly dislike and conduct a mini-mindfulness experiment!

You can either choose something relatively quick and easy to buy or prepare or, if you really want to go to town and have some fun with this, cook yourself a whole meal.

Sit down with the food in front of you. Take your time; take it in visually, explore its contours, its landscape. Note any thoughts and feelings, any 'stories' you might be telling yourself, simply allowing them to be, to come and to go. How does it smell? Can you suspend your initial judgement? Can you stay in the present moment, not anticipating how it is going to taste? Remember – you haven't even put it in your mouth yet!

When you're ready, slowly take a mouthful. Let the food sit in your mouth without chewing yet. Explore it with your tongue, both the texture and any flavour it might have before you have bitten into it. Once you've spent some time doing that, slowly start to chew. Notice how the texture and flavour start to change. Do your best to let go into the taste and texture of it, to soften around any unpleasantness. Take a few slower, longer breaths to help, and see if you can relax mindfully into the experience.

Be kind to yourself too; give yourself permission to spit the food out at any point during this mindfulness experiment! It's your choice.

Stay with the unpleasantness if you can, explore that to find out what it's really about. See whether it changes or dissipates in any way as you sit with it, stay with it, soften and relax into it.

Afterwards reflect on the experience without judging yourself in any way. What did you notice? Were you able to stay with the discomfort? Did softening and relaxing into it rather than resisting it change your experience in any way? From this small experiment, what did you learn about sitting with or bearing with something challenging?

I hope you've enjoyed dipping your toe into the clear forest pool of mindfulness in this chapter. Let's turn now to the longer, traditional practices. The first one, the Body Scan, is always a favourite with my students!

5

The classics

We don't do sitting meditation to become a Buddha or even to become enlightened. We sit to be happy. That's all.

Thich Nhat Hanh

Three main, classic meditation practices help us build our mindfulness muscles: the Body Scan; Mindfulness of Breathing; Kindly Awareness. Each will help us cultivate the qualities of mindfulness and learn the principles experientially, though each has a slightly different focus.

The Body Scan helps us become more aware of our body, connect more with it and inhabit it more fully. Along with these comes a heightened awareness of our senses, all of which, as you'll find, helps bring us into the here and now.

Mindfulness of Breathing, as the name suggests, focuses on the breath and all the sensations and movement associated with the breath. While still focusing very much on the body, it is a great practice for becoming aware of and working with our thoughts. By patiently watching the mind in action we come to know it, its fancies and foibles.

We start to come to know ourselves. We start to build the foundations for our recovery.

The third practice, Kindly Awareness (or Loving Kindness), still needs to be rooted in the body and the breath, but the focus is more on the heart, on our emotions and working with those. We're cultivating compassion, especially self-compassion at first, and an awareness of our common humanity, both of which are so essential to our healing and recovery.

For longer practices such as the ones in this chapter, it's probably best to download free audio recordings from my website or one of the others listed under 'Useful addresses and resources'. That way you can relax into them and get the most out of them.

The Body Scan

The Body Scan is primarily about body awareness, moment-by-moment awareness of the body. It's usually done lying down but can also be done seated. It has the added benefit of being very relaxing, so much so that we sometimes fall asleep during it! This is especially so if we listen to it in the evening or late at night. Some people specifically use the Body Scan to help with insomnia, and find it very beneficial.

If you do fall asleep, don't worry – you're obviously tired and need the rest. If you can manage to stay awake you will, however, get the most benefit from the practice.

One trick you can try, if you're keen to stay awake, is to bend your legs up with the soles of your feet flat on the surface or bed. If you start to fall asleep your legs will flop over to one side and gently 'nudge' you awake.

If it keeps happening, even when you listen to it earlier in the day, you may on some level be resisting the practice; your body is finding its own way of avoiding it. Explore, with gentleness, what might be going on. If you experience any restlessness, that's all right too. Simply observe it, without judgement, as best you can, bringing patient kindness to your body.

The Body Scan varies in length, usually anything from about 20 minutes to 40 minutes. If this practice is new to you, you might like to start with a shorter version and build up. If you're keen, just go for it; dive right into a longer one! Ideally we do the Body Scan once a day, every day. As with all these practices, the more we put in, the more we get out.

The following is the first part of the script from the Body Scan audio file that is available on my website (<www.catherine-g-lucas.com>). It will give you an idea of what this powerful practice involves. As I said, you'll want to download it to listen to it.

The practice

So just beginning to settle into the Body Scan making sure you've got everything you need in order to be warm and comfortable. And having a sense of giving our weight up . . . letting go, knowing that the whole planet is beneath us, supporting us . . . so we can give our full weight up to the floor, to the mattress.

We can feel the points of contact. We can feel where the body meets the surface, the back of the head . . . the back of the shoulders, the whole length of the back . . . the hips and the buttocks, the backs of the legs and the heels or the soles of the feet. Just noticing what that contact feels like. On the out-breath, just letting go a little bit more, letting ourselves sink a little bit more towards the earth.

We're going to start this Body Scan with the part of the body where we probably feel the most pressure, the most contact. This is the base of the spine, the lower back, so just noticing how this area feels.

Just allowing the lower back to spread out against the surface, letting it take as much room as it wants . . . We don't need to hold on . . . Seeing whether you can feel the very subtle movement of the breath in the base of the spine. You can probably feel that the amount of contact, the amount of pressure varies slightly as we breathe in and breathe out. So just noticing that for a moment.

Then we can begin to follow the vertebrae upwards, we can begin to follow the spine . . . We come up to the middle back, waist area. Here there's maybe less contact, less pressure and all the while the spine is rippling with the breath, the vertebrae moving in sync with each other . . . We can follow those up to the upper back, this broad expanse of the upper back . . . As we breathe in we can feel the shoulder blades. Feel them moving out, broadening out and releasing on the out-breath.

The shoulders, these big joints, we can breathe into the shoulders, just allowing them to be spacious, allowing the arms to fall from these joints. Like a puppet or a rag doll, the arms are just floppy and loose . . . So we're giving the full weight of the arms up. We can feel them as heavy. We can take our awareness down through the upper arms, down to the elbows . . . So we've got the hard, bony, outer part of the elbow, then we've got the soft smooth flesh on the inside of the elbow. The elbows resting on the surface . . . and so on.

Mindfulness of Breathing

There are many variations on this. One I find particularly helpful, and use with my students, breaks the practice up into four stages. Each stage can last 5–10 minutes, so the practice can be 20–40 minutes. It could also be shorter or longer if that suits you better. A bell is traditionally rung between each stage to mark the transition from one to the next. It can be helpful to listen to an audio recording, even if it's just for the timing of the stages. There are free recordings available that simply have the sound of a bell at evenly spaced intervals, or you can listen to a led practice, probably a good idea at first (see 'Useful addresses and resources' for details).

This practice is best done sitting in as upright and comfortable a posture as possible, on something like a dining chair, or meditation cushion if you prefer.

The practice

Take time to settle down, maybe lighting a candle if you like to do that. Bring your attention to the body, the whole body . . . Become aware of your weight resting on the chair or cushion, aware of the sitting bones connecting with the chair seat . . . Allow your body to feel heavier as you gradually let go, as you relax into this posture and this practice . . .

Stage 1

In this first stage we focus on the breath, the whole of the breath, as it moves through the body . . . the torso expanding and releasing, rising and falling . . . the shoulder blades broadening and releasing . . . We notice all the sensations and movements of the breath as it ripples through the body . . . We notice how the body breathes by itself; there is no effort involved on our part . . . When we're ready, feeling settled yet alert, we start to count each breath, quietly in our minds. We breathe in, breathe out, and count one. We breathe in, breathe out, two. We breathe in, and out, up to ten. If we get to ten we then gently start back at one again.

If, or rather when, the mind wanders off and we lose count, simply start back at one, without any sense of judgement. If you notice irritation or impatience with yourself, simply and kindly let that go. There is nothing to achieve, nothing to get right or wrong. As I mentioned before, every time we notice the mind has wandered off is actually a moment of mindfulness. We're simply observing everything that happens, the breath going in and out, the mind wandering in and out. Don't get too hung up about the counting. The practice is about the breath and noticing every single aspect of it, each tiny sensation and movement. It's not about the counting. In fact, if you prefer not to count because you find it a distraction, that's fine too.

Stage 2

We follow the same process as Stage 1, but this time we count just before each in-breath rather than after each out-breath. It's a subtle difference, enough to help keep us engaged. If you notice that your mind is tending to wander a great deal, it can help to just briefly bring your attention back to that contact with the ground, your weight in the chair or on the cushion, to your sitting bones and how they feel. When you're ready, resume the focus on the breath, and the counting if you wish to.

Stage 3

Here we drop the counting and drop down into the practice that little bit more, resting in the breath, following the breath, becoming the breath. As we breathe in we notice the sense of expansion, of spaciousness across the chest, as the lungs fill and the ribs expand. As we breathe out we let go, the lungs emptying, the ribs releasing; the mind releasing anything it's been holding on to, clinging on to.

Stage 4

Now we refine our awareness further still by focusing on one small aspect of the breath, one specific part of the body. Maybe choose somewhere in the body where you feel the breath particularly strongly or allow yourself to be simply drawn to an area you wish to focus on. In traditional practices often the focus is on the tip of the nose and all the sensations at the tip of the nose as you breathe in and out. Any part of the body where you can feel the breath is fine for this, especially an area you feel curious about, interested in. Hold your focus lightly, with intention, in that place, following the rhythm of the breath.

When you're ready bring the Mindfulness of Breathing practice to a close. Take your time to reorientate yourself.

The idea is to then take this mindful breathing with us as we go through the day. We are using this way of bringing the wandering mind back to the body, to the physical sensations, to this present moment. You can repeat Thich Nhat Hanh's simple phrases to help you stay connected to the breath, to help you stay present and mindful throughout the day:

> Breathing in, I know I'm breathing in.
> Breathing out, I know I'm breathing out.

Kindly Awareness

This is a heart-warming variation of the classic Loving Kindness meditation. I've adapted it slightly from Bowen, Chawla and Marlatt's *Mindfulness-Based Relapse Prevention for Addictive Behaviors* (pp. 153–4). You can download their free audio version of it from the MBRP website.

The practice

Start by allowing the body and mind to settle in your chosen position. Feel the weight of your body. Feel your body in the chair or on the cushion. Feel the ground beneath you, knowing that the earth, the whole planet, is supporting you right now. As you breathe out, let go of any tension you might be aware of holding in your body. Allow your body to soften – soft belly, soft face, soft jaw.

Now bring to mind someone you know personally, or know of, who is easy to love and towards whom you naturally have feelings of friendliness and caring. This may be a friend, a child, a grandchild or grandparent. Or it could be a spiritual guide or teacher, or even a pet. It's best not to pick someone with whom you've had conflict or with whom you are romantically involved, but, rather, someone towards whom you feel an easy warmth and friendliness. Maybe someone who brings a smile to your face when you simply think about him or her.

Imagine that this special someone is sitting next to you, by your side or in front of you. Don't worry if you're not able to picture this person; just allow yourself to focus on the feeling, the sensations you may experience in his or her presence. Take a few minutes to pay attention to how you feel, allowing yourself to feel compassion and caring towards him or her. Where in your body do you feel these emotions? It may be in the centre of your chest, where your heart is, or in the belly or the face. Wherever you feel the experience of caring and kindness in your body, with each breath, allow this area to soften. If you have trouble sensing this or finding the area where these feelings might be centred, it's all right. Just keep your focus on this general area of your heart and notice what, if anything, you can sense there throughout this exercise.

Now, if it feels comfortable to you, send this being well-wishes. We often use the following phrases, repeating them quietly in our minds:

> *May you be safe and protected. May you be happy. May you be peaceful. May you be free from suffering.* (Repeat slowly.)

You can use these well-wishes or you can create your own – whatever feels most genuine for you. Continue to repeat them mentally: *May you be safe and protected. May you be happy. May you be peaceful. May you live with ease.* – or whatever well-wishes you have chosen.

The idea is not to make anything happen; we are simply sending well-wishes, the way you might wish someone a safe journey or a good day. If you find yourself having thoughts such as, 'This isn't working' or 'This is silly', just notice these thoughts and gently guide your attention back to the wishes. Similarly, if you find yourself feeling frustrated or irritated, just bring your attention to that experience, and remember that you can always bring your attention back to simply sensing the area where your heart is. Remind yourself there is nothing in particular you are supposed to feel when you do this practice. Just allow your experience to be your experience.

Now imagine that this person is sending the same well-wishes back to you: *May you be safe and protected. May you be happy. May you be peaceful. May you be free from suffering*. After a little while, if it feels comfortable, shift your attention to yourself and send yourself the well-wishes: *May I be safe and protected. May I be happy. May I be peaceful. May I be free from suffering.* – or whatever wishes you have chosen. With each wish, take a moment to feel that wish in your body and heart. What does 'safe' feel like? How does 'happy' feel?

If it's easier, imagine yourself as a young child receiving these well-wishes. If you find yourself having judging thoughts or thinking about the exercise, just notice these thoughts and gently come back to the phrases. If you notice any resistance or anxiety, as best you can, allow that resistance to soften. See if you can have compassion for your experience, just as it is. Continue to experiment with this on your own for a few more minutes. When you're ready, gently bring the practice to a close. Bring your awareness fully back into the room. Maybe stretch a little. You might like to journal about how the meditation was for you, what came up or anything you learnt.

Now that you've had a chance to both have a go with the introductory practices and start practising more fully with the meditations in this chapter, let's turn to those practices tailor-made for helping you establish and maintain recovery.

6

Specific recovery practices

You can't stop the waves, but you can learn to surf.

Jon Kabat-Zinn

Now that you've started building your mindfulness muscles we can flex them by learning some applications designed especially for recovery. These are taught on the Mindfulness-Based Relapse Prevention (MBRP) and Mindfulness-Based Addiction Recovery (MBAR) courses. I've included three here: a recovery version of the three-minute breathing space known as SOBER; a practice called Urge Surfing; a self-compassion practice.

The SOBER three-minute breathing space

The three-minute breathing space is a wonderfully versatile, brief practice that can be used anytime, anywhere. It's particularly helpful when we need to pause, to take a few moments to come back to our centre, to ourselves, to regroup so to speak. I encourage students to use it throughout the day, whether they're at home, out and about, parking the car or at work. On occasion, when students feel self-conscious doing it at their desk in an open-plan office, they take themselves off and do the three-minute breathing space in the loo!

The practice

SOBER is essentially the same practice as the three-minute breathing space, but with a useful acronym to help remember its sequence. SOBER stands for:

- Stop
- Observe
- Breathe
- Expand
- Respond

Stop or **slow** down.

Wherever you are and whatever you're doing, within reason, you can stop, even for as little as 30 seconds. Waiting at traffic lights can become an opportunity to come back to yourself in this way.

Observe your thoughts, emotions and physical sensations.

Take a moment to check in with yourself. How are you doing right now? What are you aware of physically, mentally, emotionally? We don't need to change anything; we're just noticing how it is right now.

Breathe – focus your attention on the breath.

Focus on all the sensations and movement of the breath. Remember, it's through the body and the breath that we bring ourselves into the moment. Follow the breath for a few cycles or as long as you need or would like to.

Expand your awareness to the whole body and the environment you're in.

Broaden your awareness out from the breath to the whole body, to your contact with the ground, to your environment, opening your eyes if you've had them closed.

Respond – you should now be in a better position to respond with awareness rather than in a knee-jerk, reactive way.

The advantage of SOBER is that it can buy us just enough time to stop ourselves behaving in an automatic, unhelpful way. It can give us that minute or two, or three, that we need to give ourselves choice in how we respond.

This three-minute breathing space is particularly helpful for challenging times when something has just happened to upset or rile us, or something that could potentially derail our sobriety. It goes hand-in-hand with urge surfing, coming up next.

And of course it can be as short or as long as we want – anything from 30 seconds to a minute to five or even ten minutes. If you can sit down and close your eyes, so much the better. Equally it can be done standing in the queue at the supermarket. You need never waste a moment of waiting in queues again!

Urge Surfing

This is a key mindfulness practice on MBRP and MBAR programmes. It helps us cope with craving or urges by riding them like waves, allowing them to rise, crest and fall away of their own accord, without needing to do anything ourselves. We saw earlier how the smoker who cannot imagine going 45 minutes without a cigarette can actually discover that cravings can and do pass of their own accord if given the time and space to do so. Without personal, experiential proof that this works, it's difficult to trust or believe. The Buddha always said 'Don't believe my teachings; test them out for yourself.' So with Urge Surfing we can recreate real-life situations in our imaginations, and practise. Then when a situation actually arises, we're equipped and ready to handle it, to test the theory for ourselves.

Often when we're able to sit with what we find difficult, challenging or triggering, and really explore it, we learn a great deal. Part of the aim of Urge Surfing is to really step towards the craving or urge and explore it. Can you gently and kindly step towards it in this way? Where in your body do you feel it? Is it true that if you stay with it and simply watch it, without acting on it, it will get worse and worse? Or will it crest and pass, like a wave dissolving back into the sea?

The practice

Choose a scenario, either imaginary or a past one, something that you have found challenging, that might trigger and tempt you to have a drink. In this case, however, in your imagination you're *not* going to use alcohol. You're going to bring compassionate curiosity to the scenario as you explore it. Be careful not to choose a situation that would be overwhelming. If at any point during the practice it feels too much, be sure to listen to that. You can either choose a less intense situation or stop and come back to it later when you feel more resourced. This is all about being kind and gentle with yourself.

As with all the practices, as you settle down, feel your weight in the chair or on the cushion. Feel your contact with the ground. Now take your awareness to the breath, noticing any sensations, any movement, maybe feeling the expansion and release of the torso, or the abdomen. When you're ready, bring to mind the scenario you've chosen. (The practice that follows is from Bowen, Chawla and Marlatt's *Mindfulness-Based Relapse Prevention for Addictive Behaviors*, pp. 66–7.)

> [R]eally picture yourself in that place or situation or with that person. Imagining the events or situation that lead up to [it], and bringing yourself right to that point where you feel triggered, as though you might behave reactively . . . pause here for a moment. We often tend to either fall into craving or fight to resist it. Here, we are going to explore our experience a little, finding a balance, just staying with and observing the experience . . . noticing any emotions that are arising . . . thoughts . . . physical sensations . . . What does this feel like in your body? Noticing, too, what it is about this experience that feels intolerable. Can you stay with it, and be gentle with yourself? If you

begin to feel overwhelmed at any point, you can always back off a bit by allowing your eyes to open . . . Remember that we are practicing staying with this experience in a kind, curious way. We are making the choice not to act on any urges or cravings that are arising . . . just staying with them and observing, as best you can, what is happening in your body and mind, what a craving or an urge *feels* like . . . discovering what happens when you stay with this experience and explore it a little: what is it you are truly needing? Is there a longing for something? Maybe there is fear, anger, loneliness . . . Just staying with this discomfort . . . with a very gentle curiosity.

If a craving or urge becomes increasingly intense, you might imagine it like an ocean wave . . . imagine that you are riding that wave, using your breath as a surfboard to stay steady . . . Your job is to ride the wave of desire from its beginning, as it grows, staying right with it, through the peak of its intensity, keeping your balance while the wave rises, and staying on top of it until it naturally begins to subside. You are riding this wave rather than succumbing to the urge and being wiped out by it. Just watching the pattern as the urge or craving rises and then falls, and trusting that . . . all the waves of desire, like waves on the ocean, arise and fall, and eventually fade away.

Noticing now how you can simply stay present with this wave instead of immediately reacting to it. Accepting the craving and staying with it, without giving into the urge, without acting on it, without having to make it go away.

As you bring the practice to a close, gently let go of what you've been imagining. Open your eyes, maybe stretch a little. You might like to journal anything you've just learnt or realized.

Sometimes we experience a level of pain or distress that feels totally overwhelming. We can feel out of control, as if we're going to drown in it. We may not even be able to identify where it's coming from or what the cause is, especially if it's intergenerational wounding that has been passed down through the family. At times like this, when we might feel seriously tempted to reach for a drink, this Urge Surfing practice can make all the difference. It's the difference between being overwhelmed and drowning or managing to stay on top of things and surf that urge, surf that wave.

Self-compassion Practice: compassion towards the costs of our addiction

At some point in our recovery we may well come face to face with the painful reality of how our addiction has impacted on our lives and those of others. In Part 1, Brendan spoke movingly about the consequences of his alcoholic behaviour and the very painful thoughts and feelings he had around that. At first, when he started to meditate, they ran a loop in his mind.

We've already seen how important compassion – especially self-compassion – is on our mindfulness journey of recovery. This is particularly so when we're coping with the shame, guilt and more that our past behaviour brings up. In *Eight Step Recovery*, mentioned in Chapter 2, Valerie Mason-John and Dr Paramabandhu Groves suggest the following Self-compassion Practice to help deal with this. You can use it especially when you notice painful emotions coming up.

The practice

Give yourself five minutes. Settle your body and allow it to come to rest. Bring to mind one of the costs of your addiction. Allow yourself to notice the effect of bringing this to mind, especially in the body. If you find your mind is spinning off into critical thoughts, try to keep coming back to the sensations in the body, particularly in the chest or heart area. Use your breath to breathe with whatever is happening. Allow the breath to be like a friend, touching whatever is painful with compassion. Breathe with whatever pain or hurt there is, whether caused to yourself or to others. (p. 107)

After this would be another good moment to journal, to help you process anything the reflection brought up for you. Is it time for one of those oxytocin-boosting Selfie Hugs?

We're ready now to concentrate more fully on the fundamental point of mindfulness: to be able to take it with us throughout each day, throughout our interactions, our activities, our lives; to be able to be present with all that arises, no matter how challenging. As we saw in Chapter 3, Brendan commented on this aspect when he said:

> I still practise mindfulness but the context and emphasis has changed. What I mean is that even though the practice is still the same . . . I now practise it in my home, in the car, at work, etc. It is a transformative tool that travels with me.

7
Everyday mindfulness

The way we drink our tea can transform our lives if we truly devote our attention to it.

Thich Nhat Hanh

Like Brendan, who practises mindfulness in his home, in the car, at work, you too want to be able to take your meditation practice off the cushion or chair and into your whole day. So how do we do that? I've chosen having a hot drink and eating as examples. Exactly the same principles apply to any activity, whether you're cleaning your teeth or cleaning your home, having a shower or watering the plants. I've also included coping with painful thoughts and feelings that become obsessive or compulsive, as they can threaten to overwhelm us at any time of day or night. Here is a general tip before we get stuck in.

Solo-tasking

Do your best to do only one thing at a time. In the same way that with Mindful Walking or Mindful Jogging (see Chapter 8), it's best not to be plugged in to your iPod/MP3 player, that goes for everything else too. If you're on the phone, just be on the phone. Give your full attention to the person you're talking with rather than pottering about with kitchen chores, the phone wedged under your chin. Ditto for driving, walking the dog or while you're at work. Don't kid yourself that you can multi-task mindfully.

I remember one particular executive on a course of mine whose work was very busy. She was concerned that if she really practised mindfulness at work it would slow her down and she would get a lot less done. She found the exact opposite was true. Because she was more focused, she wasted a lot less time. She also found she responded to situations and challenges far more creatively.

A Mindful Hot Drink

How many times have you discovered a cold, half-drunk mug of tea or coffee? While working on this book, I've found several! This practice is about sitting down with that hot drink and actually drinking it, all of it! Here is Thich Nhat Hanh on drinking tea:

> Drinking a cup of tea is a pleasure we can give ourselves every day. To enjoy our tea, we have to be fully present and know clearly and deeply that we are drinking tea . . . The way we drink our tea can transform our lives if we truly devote our attention to it.

The practice

You can start the practice from the moment you put the kettle on. Concentrate on the process of making the drink, without allowing the mind to wander off. Hold this awareness lightly without too much effort, without forcing anything.

When you've made your drink, sit down with it. Is there steam rising off it? Sit quietly watching it, following it.

As it's cooling, notice any feelings that are coming up. If, for instance, you become aware of impatience, notice that with a sense of receptive curiosity: 'That's interesting; feelings of irritation are coming up.' Let them go without judgement. We don't need to buy into our feelings. We can just observe them and let them pass through.

When you take a sip, savour that. Hold the liquid in your mouth and notice the warmth, the flavour, before swallowing.

When you swallow, how far down do you feel the hot liquid flowing into you?

Between sips bring your attention to the breath. As you inhale and exhale, follow the whole of the breath through. As always, notice the sensations and movements of the breath. Is your collar bone rising and falling? Are your shoulders moving?

Stay as present as you can with the drink as you gradually consume it. What do you discover when you bring your full attention to a hot drink in this way?

If the mind feels busy, just do your best to keep coming back to the physical sensations, back to the breath. Whether the mind is chatty or settled, you're still practising mindfulness. Be aware of any tendency to judge 'busy' as 'bad', 'settled' as 'good'. It all simply is how it is.

As you sit in stillness with your drink, know that you're sitting with yourself. This is time you're giving to you.

As you come to the end of your drink, be aware of how you transition into your next activity. Notice to what extent you're able to take any mindfulness with you into that. Again, simply note that with compassionate curiosity.

A Mindful Mouthful

Our very first practice, Raspberry Relish, will have given you a sense of what mindful eating involves; the aromas, the texture, the taste, even the colours. Many of us rush our food in our busy, stressed lives just to get on to the next activity. In mindful eating we slow the process down.

One of my mindfulness students would eat his breakfast on the go. He'd have a bowl of cereal and as he was getting ready for work he would have a spoonful here and there, without actually sitting down to eat it. It wasn't long, however, before he decided he no longer wanted to do that. He chose eating a Mindful Bowlful as part of his daily practice and realized that breakfast wasn't about getting from here to there, to just get it over and done with, but was about being here, now.

The practice

Eating more mindfully often means eating more slowly. You might want to try it with something like a salad at first, so that you don't end up with cold food! Alternatively, go for something piping hot like a soup, so that you're obliged to eat it slowly! Choose a meal that you can eat alone, so that you can concentrate. Alternatively, try what my husband and I do: when we want to eat more mindfully, we agree to eat in silence. That might feel a bit odd at first, but it makes for a more special meal, a shared meal in a different way.

Get ready now to savour that flavour!

Before you start eating, take a few moments to look at the food in front of you. Take it in. What do you notice about it? How does it smell?

When you feel focused and settled, take your first mouthful. Chew it slowly and thoroughly.

As you swallow the food, notice the sensations in your throat.

Make sure you've swallowed that mouthful *before* loading up your fork or spoon with the next. Very often we tend to be ready to shovel the next mouthful in the second we've swallowed the previous one, or even before sometimes.

Watch to see what your habitual tendencies around eating are.

If you would like to, you can actually put your cutlery down in between mouthfuls and have fun playing with that.

You might not want to eat slowly and mindfully all the time, but by choosing certain meals to practise with, your awareness of eating will be increased overall. You'll become much more aware of when you're rushing your food, of when any stress is playing out in your eating. You'll also notice more readily when you're eating on autopilot and barely becoming aware of the flavours. The moment we notice these things we have choice. We can choose to do it differently. Remember not to judge yourself. All we're doing is noticing how it is.

Coping with obsessive, compulsive thinking

Sometimes something will happen that has a lot of emotional charge for us. We'll find ourselves going over and over in our minds a particular situation or conversation. We can't seem to get rid of it; our thinking becomes compulsive, obsessive. These are challenges that really put our mindfulness to the test. The first thing is to realize and acknowledge that we're suffering. Consciously look for ways to be kind to yourself, to practise that self-compassion we've been cultivating. Then have a go at the following.

The practice

Drop down into the body, out of the mind. What are you aware of physically? Whereabouts in the body are you feeling the emotional charge? Can you stay with that, watch that, soften around it?

Bring your awareness to your contact with the ground. Really sense into that. Notice what it feels like. Allow yourself to feel rooted to the ground, like a tree.

Take your awareness to the breath and notice how that is. What quality or word describes it? Follow it for a few cycles, or for as long as you need to.

You may find that you manage to let go of the obsessive, charged thoughts and feelings for a few minutes or even a few hours, but then they resurface again. Patiently go through the same process as above.

Do that as many times as you need to; just keep patiently and tenderly working at it. The more practised you become, the more quickly you'll be able to let go of something charged when it arises. Sometimes we can simply, firmly but kindly say to ourselves 'Stop it!'

Here is what Thich Nhat Hanh writes in *Love Letter to the Earth* about how to cope at such times:

> When we feel that we're fragile, not stable or solid, we can come back to ourselves and take refuge in the Earth. With each step we can feel her solidity beneath our feet. When we're truly in touch with the Earth, we can feel her supportive embrace and her stability. We use all our body and our mind to go back to the Earth and surrender ourselves to her. With each breath we release all our agitation, our fragility, and our suffering. Just being aware of her benevolent presence can already bring relief. (p. 26)

Other techniques

With the introductory practices you had an opportunity to have a go at 'noting' while sitting quietly; mentally noting whatever arises. There is a version of this you can do during the day, which I find very helpful in staying present. It involves a running commentary on whatever you're doing; for example: 'taking sweater off', 'opening window', 'filling kettle', 'putting kettle on', 'getting mug out', 'putting tea-bag in mug' and so on.

This applies exactly the same principle as the Noting practice: when we intentionally bring awareness to what we're doing we become more consciously aware of it. We can't be daydreaming, on autopilot, dwelling on the past or worrying about the future. It stops the mind running riot.

Remembering to remember

The trick with taking our mindfulness practice through the day is remembering to do it. The mindfulness itself becomes relatively easy if we can just remember to do it! For this reason, I encourage my students, when they're learning, to use 'reminders'. Some put a sticky note on the bathroom mirror. Others tie a rubber band around the handle of their toothbrush. If I want to remember to practise at mealtimes, I leave a note on the dining table. I could equally put one of my figures of the Buddha in the middle of the table. Find your own creative, fun way of nudging your memory.

Keeping it going

To create a varied practice, choose something you do at least once a day, preferably two or three times a day, and focus on that for a week. The following week you can choose a different activity. If you really want to go for it, choose several.

Thich Nhat Hanh also recommends dedicating one day a week to mindfulness practice. For instance, on a Sunday you could create your own personal mini-retreat. It might include a mindful walk in nature, cooking mindfully and eating in silence, taking time to sit down with a cup of tea and doing nothing but drinking that cup of tea.

During the week, starting your day mindfully helps you throughout the rest of the day. If you can deliberately punctuate the day with mindful activities, from your shower and breakfast in the morning, to a three-minute breathing space after you've parked the car at work, to regular breaks from the computer screen, to a mindful cup of tea when you get home from work and cooking dinner mindfully, then you'll be doing extremely well!

The ultimate inspiration

If you want to be inspired as to just how far you can take your daily mindfulness practice, I highly recommend the book *Knee Deep in Grace* by Amy Schmidt. Dipa Ma was a lay practitioner, as opposed to a Buddhist nun, who took mindfulness in daily life all the way.

Having suffered hugely earlier in life, Dipa Ma went on to inspire many others and still does today. Anyone who has been through huge suffering, like her, has a certain ripeness for the kind of profound transformation she experienced. Her message is very simple: 'The whole path of mindfulness is this: whatever you are doing, be aware of it.'

8

Mindful movement

Each mindful step taken with awareness is a step taken in freedom.

Thich Nhat Hanh

When we're sitting or lying still for one of the classic mindfulness practices, there is nevertheless movement, albeit subtle. The body is naturally in motion as the breath flows through it. The practice involves following that movement, those sensations and all the subtleties of that in the body. Throughout the rest of the day the body's movements are more pronounced. As we learn to watch the subtle movements in the formal practices, we become more adept at following those coarser movements as we go through our day.

Any kind of movement or exercise is a particularly good time to practise mindfulness. The physicality helps us connect with the body and come into the present moment through the physical sensations.

I've included two examples of mindful movement here. Mindful Walking, or Walking Meditation, is a recognized, traditional mindfulness practice, often used on retreat. Mindful Jogging is also a form of exercise that is easily accessible. These are everyday activities, like the ones we looked at in the last chapter, that can become part of your mindfulness practice. The same principles and qualities apply to whatever movement or exercise you do, even walking up the stairs. Don't miss an opportunity to practise!

Yoga is often the practice of choice on mindfulness courses. Other gentle forms such as Chi Gung also lend themselves well. By their very nature and slow pace they make excellent mindful movement practices. Any exercise you enjoy, from hiking to climbing, from dancing to swimming, and everything in between, can become part of your mindfulness practice.

If you have restricted mobility, for example if you're a wheelchair user, then I recommend the mindful movement practices developed by Vidyamala Burch and the Breathworks team. Vidyamala suffered spinal injuries in her late teens and early twenties and is a wheelchair user herself. The exercises are designed specifically for those with physical conditions and injuries. You can find them in her book *Living Well with Pain and Illness* (see 'References and further reading').

Mindful Walking

No other mindfulness teacher is more associated with Mindful Walking than the Vietnamese monk Thich Nhat Hanh. He writes beautifully about it in *Love Letter to the Earth*:

> Walking meditation is a way of waking up to the wonderful moment we are living in. If our mind is caught, preoccupied with our worries and our suffering, or if we distract ourselves with other things [like talking or eating] while walking, we can't really practice mindfulness; we can't enjoy the present moment. We're missing out on life. But if we're awake, then we'll see this is a wonderful moment that life has given us, the only moment in which life is available. (p. 96)

Here are some of his simple instructions:

> When you walk, don't think about anything else. Most of us have a radio constantly playing in our head tuned to the station Radio NST, Radio Nonstop Thinking. Most of this thinking is unproductive thinking. The more we think the less available we are to what is around us. Therefore we have to learn to turn off the radio and stop our thinking in order to fully enjoy the present moment. When walking you just walk, giving one hundred percent of your awareness and attention to your walking. (p. 51)

So how do we do it? How do we stop the endless inner chatter? The trick is to keep coming back to the body, keep coming back to physical sensations. When you're focusing on the texture of the ground beneath your foot, you can't also be planning what to eat for lunch.

The practice

If you've not tried Mindful Walking before you might like to start with just five minutes, building up to ten minutes, even fifteen minutes. Whenever possible, always do this practice barefoot – you can feel so much more that way. Choose different surfaces on different days. Notice how the different textures feel underfoot. Do the practice as slowly . . . as . . . you . . . possibly . . . can. Then another time experiment with varying the speed. This example is based on walking on grass. Enjoy!

During the practice, stay as focused as you can on the physical sensations of walking, saving admiring the flowers, trees, wildlife for another time. Start by taking your awareness to your feet. What sensations can you feel?

How spongy is the grass? Does your foot sink down and then sink down some more, even further? On a particularly mossy lawn, notice how when you first put your weight down very gently on one foot it sinks into the soft spongy moss a little. Then, as you put more weight down on that foot, you sink in even more, even deeper, as the moss gives way beneath the sole of your foot.

How do the tips of the grass feel in that moment when the sole of your foot is hovering over the grass before putting your weight down?

Notice your toes. How do they help support you, balance you?

Does the grass push up between your toes? Always gently bring the mind back if it wanders off.

If you would like to, stay totally focused on your feet, really getting into the rhythm of taking one step, followed by another, followed by another . . .

Alternatively, you can also gradually start taking your awareness upwards, noticing the ankles and the flexing of those bones.

Then the calves and shins, feeling the changing sensations in the muscles, then the knees, the thighs, the big muscles in the thighs, the hips.

Notice also how there's not only a forward movement in walking; there's also a side to side motion in the hips. You might like to allow your attention to settle on that and follow that for a while.

When you're ready to bring the practice to a close, you can set your intention to take the mindfulness you've been cultivating with you into your next activity.

Mindful Jogging

On a personal note

I never really managed to get into jogging. I tried a couple of times and although I kept it up for a few weeks or even months, I wasn't able to sustain it. It was always a slog. I'd always be pushing through resistance until eventually that resistance got the better of me and I'd give up altogether.

Until, that is, I became a mindfulness practitioner. That completely changed my attitude. I learnt to follow my body, take my lead from it, rather than try to make my body do something it didn't want to. With mindfulness, I discovered the huge difference between pushing my body to go further or for longer (as in 5–10 minutes!) and running because I wanted to, because I was enjoying it and because I could run for 20–30 minutes almost effortlessly (on the flat!).

If I had to sum up what changed, I think it's that I simply let go. Instead of being all about striving and pushing, it has become all about a gentle, light, easy stride. I gave myself permission to stop and walk whenever I wanted to, and within a week I found I no longer needed to or wanted to. There is a sense of being kind to my body rather than punishing it. It is no longer about goals, about how far or how long I can run for, but all about being in the moment, basking in the natural surroundings I'm running through, being with my body rather than against it. I must admit, I also read *Born to Run* by Christopher McDougall (see 'References and further reading'), which I found hugely inspiring and motivating. I challenge anyone to read that book and not want to get out there and run!

Alan Marlatt (see Chapter 3) and colleagues also did some research with interesting findings for jogging. They selected a group of heavy social drinkers to see what impact different practices would have on reducing drinking rates. Over a 16-week period, the three variables were meditation practice, muscle relaxation and running, alongside a control group. On average, consumption rates dropped 50 per cent.

What is more, participants carried on of their own accord during the follow-up period: 62 per cent of the runners and 57 per cent of the meditators carried on practising regularly. So if you are both a jogger and a meditator, that's a win-win. And if you can meditate while you're jogging, there'll be no stopping you!

The practice

As with Mindful Walking, if you can do it barefoot, I highly recommend it. Realistically, that may only be possible along the beach. To help the sense of inner stillness, you might like to jog at a time of day that is generally quite quiet and still, such as first thing in the morning. You can meditate beforehand, for example the Mindfulness of Breathing practice, to help you settle the mind and get focused.

The following is based on running barefoot along the beach.

Before you start jogging, take a few moments to ground yourself, feel the earth beneath you, feel your feet firmly planted on it. Take a few breaths; notice the movements and sensations of the breath.

If you like to warm up and do any stretches, really focus on your muscles as you do those. What do you notice? Does one calf feel different from the other, for instance?

When you're ready, set off at a light, easy pace.

As with Mindful Walking, bring your attention to the feet first. How does the surface feel beneath the soles? If you're running barefoot on sand, how does the texture of the sand feel? Dry and soft or wet and firm?

Is your foot sinking slightly into the sand? A lot? How does that feel? What about the temperature of the sand?

You can then stay focused on the feet or gradually move up the legs and up the body.

Take time also to notice the breath. What word or adjective would you use to describe it? Easy? Laboured? Flowing? Staccato? How does this change as you continue to run?

As with all meditation practices, simply bring the mind back when it goes off at a tangent. It may do that more the longer you jog for. Or you may find that you're able to get more and more focused.

Whatever happens, don't judge it. There's no right or wrong, good or bad. It just is. All constantly changing, all constantly in motion. All you have to do is witness all that is.

A deeper connection

There is another dimension to Mindful Walking that I feel applies equally to Mindful Jogging. With these practices there is a sense in which we're connecting with far more than just ourselves in the present moment, we're connecting with something much bigger, much deeper. As Thich Nhat Hanh puts it in *Love Letter to the Earth*:

> While practicing mindful walking, we have a chance to enter into deep communion with the planet Earth . . . Every step placed softly, gently and mindfully on Mother Earth can bring us a lot of healing and happiness. (p. 62)

Whether we're walking or jogging we can tread lightly on her. Thich Nhat Hanh writes movingly:

> Dear Mother Earth,
> . . . Every time I place my feet on the Earth I have a chance to be in touch with you and with all your wonders . . . Each mindful and gentle step can nourish me, heal me, and bring me into contact with myself and with you in the present moment. (p. 108)

Ultimately, as well as connecting with and caring more for our planet, through our mindfulness practice we can connect with our shared, common humanity. As we step towards and heal our own pain, our own suffering, so we step towards that of others. Our recovery ripples out over the still forest pool, reaching all those whose lives we touch.

Dive in!

Make mindfulness an integral part of your recovery and you won't be just dipping your toe in that pool of mindfulness. You'll be bathing in it! Your recovery will become unassailable. To paraphrase Achaan Chah, practise a little and you'll find a little peace. Practise a lot and you'll find a lot of peace. Practise totally, let your practice become your life, and you'll find total peace. There is nothing to stop you diving in and reaping the benefits of the extraordinary life transformation mindfulness can bring.

Go well on your journey to health and wholeness. Happy bathing!

Useful addresses and resources

Courses

Mindfulness-Based Addiction Recovery (MBAR)
Breathing Space
The London Buddhist Centre
51 Roman Road
Bethnal Green
London E2 0HU
Tel: 0845 458 4716
www.breathingspacelondon.org.uk

Mindfulness-Based Relapse Prevention (MBRP)
Action on Addiction
Head Office
East Knoyle
Salisbury
Wiltshire SP3 6BE
Tel: 0300 330 0659
Website: www.actiononaddiction.org.uk

Look for a mindfulness course in your area, such as MBRP or MBAR, that is designed specifically for alcohol recovery. If there isn't one, a more general mindfulness course is the next best alternative, as long as you have other support in place. Ideally you'll have other support alongside your mindfulness training anyway, but this is particularly important if the course isn't a dedicated one.

Audio recordings

Free Body Scan practice (22 mins): <www.catherine-g-lucas.com>.

Free mindfulness audio recordings, including Urge Surfing, SOBER and kindness practices available in both male and female voices: <www.mindfulrp.com>.

Free mindfulness audio recordings, including meditation bells and ten-minute practices, such as the Body Scan and Mindfulness of Breathing: <www.freemindfulness.org>.

Other resources

5th Precept Sangha
<www.5th-precept.org>
Buddhist-based practices for abstinence and recovery from alcohol and other drug addiction. A peer-led organization; includes sitting groups around the UK.

Buddhist Recovery Network
<www.buddhistrecovery.org>
Includes a listing of meetings in the UK.

Mindfulness-Based Relapse Prevention
<www.mindfulrp.com>
For details of MBRP qualified trainers in the UK see: <www.mindfulrp.com/For-Clients.html>.

References and further reading

Bowen, Sarah, Chawla, Neha and Marlatt, G. Alan (2011) *Mindfulness-Based Relapse Prevention for Addictive Behaviors: A clinician's guide*, New York: Guilford Press.

Brand, Russell (2014) *Revolution*, London: Random House.

Burch, Vidyamala (2008) *Living Well with Pain and Illness: The mindful way to free yourself from suffering*, London: Piatkus.

Chah, Achaan, compiled by Jack Kornfield and Paul Breiter (1985) *A Still Forest Pool: The insight meditation of Achaan Chah*, Wheaton, IL: Theosophical Publishing House.

Cowell, Philip (2016) *Keeping a Journal*, London: Sheldon Press.

Grof, Christina (1993) *The Thirst for Wholeness: Attachment, addiction, and the spiritual path*, New York: HarperSanFrancisco.

Kabat-Zinn, Jon (1990) *Full Catastrophe Living: Using the wisdom of your body and mind to face stress, pain, and illness*, New York: Dell Publishing.

Lucas, Catherine G. (2015) *Coping with a Mental Health Crisis: Seven steps to healing*, London: Sheldon Press.

McDougall, Christopher (2009) *Born to Run: The hidden tribe, the ultra-runners, and the greatest race the world has never seen*, London: Profile Books.

Mason-John, Valerie and Groves, Paramabandhu (2013) *Eight Step Recovery: Using the Buddha's teachings to overcome addiction*, Cambridge: Windhorse Publications.

Maté, Gabor (2009) *In the Realm of Hungry Ghosts: Close encounters with addiction*, Toronto: Vintage Canada.

Neff, Kristin (2011) *Self Compassion: Stop beating yourself up and leave insecurity behind*, London: Hodder & Stoughton.

Nhat Hanh, Thich (1991) *The Miracle of Mindfulness: A manual on meditation*, London: Rider.

Nhat Hanh, Thich (2013) *Love Letter to the Earth*, Berkeley, CA: Parallax Press.

Schmidt, Amy (2003) *Knee Deep in Grace: The extraordinary life and teaching of Dipa Ma*, Lake Junaluska, NC: Present Perfect Books.
Williams, R. E. and Kraft, J. S. (2012) *The Mindfulness Workbook for Addiction: A guide to coping with the grief, stress and anger that trigger addictive behaviors*, Oakland, CA: New Harbinger Publications.